Comparative Literature

FRENCH LITERATURE
IN THE NINETEENTH CENTURY

Christopher Robinson

DAVID & CHARLES
Newton Abbot   London   Vancouver

BARNES & NOBLE
(a division of Harper & Row Publishers, Inc)

British Library Cataloguing in Publication Data

Robinson, Christopher
 French literature in the nineteenth century
 —(Comparative literature).
 1. French literature—19th century—History and
 criticism 2. French literature—20th century—
 History and criticism
 I. Title II. Series
 840′.9   PQ281

ISBN 0-7153-7498-2 (Great Britain)

ISBN 0-06-495943-0 (United States)
Library of Congress Catalog Card Number: 77-79571

© Christopher Robinson 1978

This edition first published in 1978
in Great Britain by
David & Charles (Publishers) Limited
Brunel House Newton Abbot Devon

First published in the USA by
Harper & Row Publishers Inc
Barnes & Noble Import Division

Published in Canada by
Douglas David & Charles Limited
1875 Welch Street North Vancouver BC

Set in 11 on 13pt Garamond
and printed in Great Britain
by Latimer Trend & Company Ltd Plymouth

Contents

CONTENTS

Preface

To survey nineteenth-century French literature on a chronological basis, or by authors and movements, would be to follow a
sound but well-worn path through familiar terrain. To attempt to
regroup its major features under any system of thematic headings
has, on the other hand, the disadvantage of disguising natural
relationships which a chronological or biographical approach
makes plain. None the less, the second method has advantages
analogous with those which Jean Cocteau proposed for the trans-
lation of the classics, in a prefatory note to his adaptation of the
Antigone (1922):

> It is tempting to photograph Greece from an aeroplane. You
> discover a completely new view of it. That is why I wanted to
> translate *Antigone*. From a bird's eye view, aspects of great beauty
> disappear, others come surging up. Unexpected juxtapositions,
> blocks, shadows, angles, reliefs are formed.

It is with this hope of creating new angles of vision that I have
tried to select thematic groupings which, while representing
fundamental tendencies of the age, also bring out relationships
between writers and writings not always considered together. The
survey is articulated around two main oppositions of values:
first, that between idealists and the portraitists of the pursuit of
ideals on the one hand, and pragmatists and the chroniclers of

7

material surfaces on the other; second, that between visionaries who believed in the paramountcy of the inner self, and collectivists who sought to subordinate the individual to religious and social movements based on group and hierarchy. It can, of course, be fairly said that the clash between pragmatism and idealism has been present in almost every age in Western European history. But it became of outstanding importance in the nineteenth century, not only because of the crisis of values caused by the social cataclysm of the end of the previous century, but also because continued progress in the sciences undermined belief in accepted notions of reality itself.

In pursuing these tensions between illusion and reality, subjectivity and collectivity, I have not abandoned chronology, and have undertaken the examination of authors individually where such an approach seemed appropriate. At times features of the landscape familiar to some will appear to have received scant, if any, attention. The selection is not wilful. Certain authors famous in their day are no longer read (Michelet, the Goncourt brothers). Some, like George Sand, are notorious for their private lives, while their books have rightly fallen into obscurity. Others are remembered for minor works rather than for what they saw as their major achievements. Sainte-Beuve may still be read for *Volupté*, but not for his literary criticism; to give the latter space here would be like regarding Sir Arthur Quiller-Couch as an indispensable figure for any introduction to English literature. The criteria for inclusion are: that an author's work has shown surviving literary merit, or that it is essential to an understanding of some major intellectual or aesthetic development of the time. It is to be hoped that, if, in the process of adopting a new perspective, great beauties *have* disappeared, others will have come surging up, such that the overflight will have seemed worthwhile.

Introduction

> ... the world, which seems
> To lie before us like a land of dreams,
> So various, so beautiful, so new,
> Hath really neither joy, nor love, nor light,
> Nor certitude, nor peace, nor help for pain;
> And we are here as on a darkling plain
> Swept with confused alarms of struggle and flight,
> Where ignorant armies clash by night.
> (Matthew Arnold 'Dover Beach')

Arnold's words serve very well to sum up the cultural and philosophical confusion into which the French Revolution and its aftermath plunged intellectual society in France. What the Revolution did, in effect, was to discredit the approach to life which was associated with the thinkers of the eighteenth-century Enlightenment, an approach which had itself undermined the traditional concepts of moral and metaphysical authority that had remained relatively unchanged since the Middle Ages. Until the mid-eighteenth century two major concepts in particular had not seriously been challenged. Firstly, that eternal truths about the nature of the universe and of man exist, if only man can establish them. Secondly, that the structure of the universe can be represented by an hierarchical system of relationships, of which an eternal principle forms the apex. Permanent ethical values thus exist independently of man, and it is the task of the theologian or philosopher, acting in the interests of mankind in general, to establish them, so that the individual may conform as nearly as possible to the abstract standard.

The so-called *philosophes*, a group of thinkers in the latter part of the eighteenth century, working in the name of reason and drawing on a wide range of recent scientific enquiry, notably the work of the Englishmen Newton and Locke, raised doubts about the nature of man's place in the universe. Their doubts were not necessarily intended to undermine the validity of either of the concepts outlined above, but they did serve to put a new importance on man himself rather than on abstractions existing independently of man. Whether, like Voltaire, they approved of reason and science as the sole arbiters of truth, or, like Rousseau, they promoted the value of intuition, whether like the deists they believed that God was a remote metaphysical principle, or like Diderot they doubted the need to postulate the existence of a God at all, they were all convinced of the significance of man, and of the possibility of his moral perfection. The Revolution seemed to offer the opportunity for man's rebirth, by its eradication of those social ills which were thought to be preventing the realisation of his progress. But the Revolution came and went, and there was nothing in its aftermath to suggest that the state of man had moved one wit closer to perfection than before. Indeed, the behaviour of man to man during the Terror suggested that there was very little basis at all for supposing that man was naturally moral; or, if he were, then society had corrupted him irredeemably.

Post-Revolutionary society found itself, therefore, in a serious choas of values. The *philosophes* had disposed of the old certainties; they had not succeeded in substituting any new ones. It is hardly surprising, then, that the primary characteristic of early nineteenth-century thought is revolt: the abandonment of all attempts to universalise, a fundamental disbelief in systems of any sort, the rejection of all solutions to human problems based on the primacy of reason. This is not to say that the existence of absolute values was universally denied, or reason totally excluded from a role in human life. It was man's capacity to attain a knowledge of absolute values, especially by purely rational processes, that was doubted. If man was to progress, it could only be intuitively, tentatively, towards some distant undefinable metaphysical goal, quite unobtainable in this material existence. Such a relapse into intuition and subjectivity was not total. But the new systematisers, the Positivists, had to take its existence into account, and it was, in any case, thirty years or more into the century before their doctrines gained much headway.

A negative principle such as revolt necessarily leads to very disparate positive manifestations. Some thinkers remained in a state of despair. Others postulated solipsistic solutions applicable only to the individual or to an élite. Social thinking tended to be utopian, philosophy metaphysical. Above all there was a constant reiteration of dissatisfaction with the material world, with what man could achieve in the material world, with the information offered to man by the material world. As Gérard de Nerval perceptively described it in his short story *Sylvie* (1853):

> We lived then in strange times, like those which usually follow upon revolutions or the decline of great reigns . . . It was a mixture of activity, hesitation, and idleness, of brilliant utopias, religious or philosophical aspirations and vague enthusiasms, mingled with certain feelings of rebirth; boredom, past discords, uncertain hopes . . . But ambition was not appropriate to our youth, and the avid hunt that was then going on for positions and honours kept us at a distance from all possible spheres of active life. All we had left for a refuge was the poet's ivory tower where we climbed ever higher and higher to escape from the crowd . . . Finally we breathed in the pure air of solitude, drank oblivion from the golden goblet of legend, became intoxicated upon poetry and love. Love, alas! Indistinct shapes, shades of pink and blue, metaphysical fantoms!

It was the age *par excellence* of the grand battle from which few ages are entirely exempt: the struggle between illusion and reality.

CHAPTER 1

The Idealist Revolt

An important way in which men expressed their dissatisfaction with the limitations apparent in the physical world was by returning to religion. Return is perhaps not quite the right term, for though the religious revival was facilitated by Napoleon's desire to rehabilitate the Church as a political institution it was to religion as a metaphysical yardstick by which man could measure morality that educated society was drawn. The beginning of the process can be seen even in a relatively orthodox figure like Joseph Joubert (1754–1824), who, in his *Thoughts*, described religion as 'the poetry of the heart', and defined 'to live' as 'to think and feel one's soul'. Here is the key to religious attitudes in the early decades of the nineteenth century. Instinct, emotion, spiritual exaltation are cultivated as the basis for faith; cult, dogma and the trappings of institutional religion are largely ignored.

The most influential force in establishing this attitude in the public mind was probably François-René de Chateaubriand (1768–1848). The majority of his major works—*Le Génie du Christianisme, Les Martyrs, La Vie de Rancé*—have overtly religious themes. Even the autobiographical *Mémoires d'Outre-Tombe*, written over a period of thirty and more years, are dominated by the view that, though man changes and no two centuries are the same,

13

he keeps his eternal condition, and is governed by a providential justice which imposes expiation and sacrifice in the wake of evil. But none of Chateaubriand's works embodies a religious approach reliant upon orthodox dogma. Significantly, the dominant (third) section of *Le Génie du Christanisme* is given over to 'the moral and poetic beauties of the Christian religion', the contribution of religion to the growth of poetry, literature in general and the fine arts. The work expounds the view that the doctrine and cult of Christianity blend excellently with the emotions of the heart and the presence of nature, aspects stressed by Chateaubriand again in his *Défense du 'Génie du Christianisme'*. Furthermore, the most read and most influential sections were not the theoretical defence of dogma, doctrine and cult, but the illustrations of moral and emotional effects, particularly the two short tales, *Atala* and *René*, which were both published separately from the main body of the work, the first in 1801, the second in 1805.

In the preface to the first edition of *Atala*, Chateaubriand wrote: 'There are no adventures in *Atala*. It is a sort of poem, half descriptive, half dramatic, wholly taken up with the portrait of two lovers walking and conversing together in solitude, wholly given over to the portrayal of the turmoil of love amid the calm of the wilderness, the calm of religion.' *René* is similarly defined as 'a train of thought' and 'a portrait of the flux of the passions, with no admixture of adventures'. They are, then, less stories than tone-poems, pieces of lyrical prose designed to create a sympathetic emotional response. But what a curious advertisement for Christianity they present! Atala, the beautiful Red Indian maiden, commits suicide rather than marry her beloved, Chactas, because she has sworn an oath to her dying mother to remain chaste. René leads an aimless existence of melancholy drifting, on the brink of suicide, until he is driven to emigrate by the loss of his sister, Amélie, who had gone into a convent in order to resist the temptations of an incestuous passion for him. Both tales, it is true, have their overt Christian message. Father Aubry,

14

the old missionary, tells the dying Atala that she, her mother, and the priest who administered the original oath of perpetual virginity offer a terrible example of the effects of excessive enthusiasm in matters of religion. The passions should be restrained by reason. Father Souël rebukes René for his attempt to be self-sufficient. Solitude, he observes, is bad for those who do not live in God. It strengthens the forces of the soul while depriving them of any object on which to exercise themselves. A man should employ himself for the good of his fellows in society. But, in each case, the message is submerged under the main effect of the tale.

The vision of religion which lingers with the reader is not one of reasoning upon gospel teachings. The name of Christ is singularly absent; both priests might as well be Socinians, given their lack of interest in specifically Christian matters. Indeed, Father Aubry defines his teaching to the Indians almost without reference to metaphysics of any kind: 'I have not given them any law, I have merely taught them to love one another, to pray to God, and to hope in a better life to come: all the laws of the world are encompassed therein.' The theme is the Rousseauesque one that man is innocent until corrupted by society. The mission Indians, raised in a good community, retain their innocence. And the mission, with its fields and simple cemetery, is an Arcadian dream; when, in the epilogue, it comes into contact with reality in the form of an attack by Cherokees, it is destroyed. A truly Christian society does not seem possible on earth. The focus of the tale is not, in any case, on the figure of the priest and his teachings. The main dramatic force derives from the tension within Atala herself, torn between her religious obedience and her earthly love for Chactas. Alongside this, and almost as powerful a distraction for the reader, is the repeated lyrical evocation of wilderness and solitude. At the very most it could be said that a sense of religious awe grows from the supernatural intervention of the storm at the moment when Atala's control over her passion finally breaks. Similarly silence, the appeasement of the storm, heralds the entry of the priest, man of God. Such effects can be called religious in the general sense of conveying an awareness of the numinous. But Christian? Scarcely.

The pattern is repeated in *René*. Religion is only one of a number of equal elements summed up by the hero himself when he is talking of the innocence of childhood: 'Each tremor of the bronze bell brought to my simple mind the innocence of rural ways, the calm of solitude, the charm of religion and the delightful melancholy of the memories of my earliest childhood.' All the appeal of religion is located in its power to calm troubled souls. René experiences the vanity of the world in his pursuit of external knowledge. He visits the sites of antiquity, the cities of the living (London) and the grandeur of nature (Etna). He explores literature and architecture. He attempts to live a normal social life. But all these experiences prove useless: 'The study of the world had taught me nothing, and I had lost the sweetness of ignorance.' For what he lacks, we are told, is God. God, but not Christ. Indeed, the only proof of religion in the book is the emotional reaction of the young René to his dead father's face: 'My father's features had, in the coffin, taken on a sublime air . . . Why should not death, who is omniscient, have engraved on the forehead of its victim the secrets of another universe?' Why should there not be in the tomb some great vision of eternity? What is expressed is a mystic awareness of supernatural forces—again, religious in a broad sense but not specifically Christian.

In the work of Chateaubriand, what happens is that religion is expressed in images which represent the emotional value of the religious experience for the writer's self. Catholicism is a collection of echoes struck in the writer by dogma and religious history on the one hand, and by literature, art and nature on the other. The validity of this symbolic idea of the 'echo' is expressed with literal clarity in a non-religious context; Chateaubriand wrote in his account of his visit to the site of ancient Sparta, in *L'Itinéraire de Paris à Jerusalem*:

A mixture of admiration and pain checked my steps and my train of thought; the silence around me was profound; I wanted at least to set an echo going in this place where the human voice was no longer heard, and I cried with all my strength 'Leonidas'. None of the ruins gave back this great name, and Sparta itself seemed to have forgotten it.

Religion, unlike the ruins of Sparta, gave back a thousand echoes, which are to be found embodied in those trappings of Catholicism that intrude the most on a Chateaubriand text—bells, organs, cathedrals, the hollow ring of the tomb. Despite his frequent insistence that he was promoting thought, not emotionalism, and that he had always recommended the submission of the passions to the control of God, Chateaubriand betrays his own awareness that emotionalism is essential to his religious response when he writes in *Le Génie du Christianisme*: 'That is the advantage of our faith over those of antiquity. The Christian religion is a wind from heaven which sets the sails of virtue billowing and builds up the storms of conscience around vice.' It is exaltation, not reason, which is the guiding force of his own religious feelings, something very close to what Mme de Staël recommends in *De l'Allemagne*. Small wonder that Louis XVIII was apocryphally attributed with the remark 'All those great servants of the altar hardly go anywhere near it. I should like to know the name of M. de Chateaubriand's confessor.' That aspect of Christianity had little appeal for him.

It seems a short step from Chateaubriand's religiosity to that of Alphonse-Marie-Louis Lamartine de Prat, though in Lamartine's case the heterodoxy led to two of his works, *Jocelyn* and *La Chute d'un ange*, being placed on the Index. If, however, we take the two writers at their closest—in their accounts of their visits to the Holy Land—the difference is marked. Chateaubriand in his *Itinéraire* goes through the motions of referring to the Old Testament and the Gospels, even if his best writing is still kept for evoking solitude and wilderness. Lamartine, in his *Voyage en*

Orient, devotes himself to a general philosophising in which the Christian elements are barely distinct. The poetry confirms this view. In the *Méditations poétiques* we find a man affected by the mystery of the world's existence, by the horror of annihilation in death, and by the apparent scandal of the triumph of evil in the material world. Accordingly, he accepts God, because he has an emotional need of a divine concept, worrying neither about his nature, nor how or why he manifests his existence. The temptation of doubt is there, the weakness of reason to deal with it is noted. Yet doubt is simply rejected as impossible. In 'Immortality' the voices of materialist philosophers raise their arguments against the poet's conviction that the soul of his beloved will live after death. He replies:

> *Qu'un autre vous réponde, ô sages de la terre.*
> *Laissez-moi mon erreur: j'aime, il faut que j'espère.*
> *Notre faible raison se trouble et se confond:*
> *Oui, la raison se tait; mais l'instinct vous répond.*

[Let someone else reply to you, sages of the earth. Leave me to my error. I am in love, so I must have hope. Our weak reason is troubled and confused. Yes, reason is silent; but instinct answers you.]

Belief is instinctive. There is a God, he is in some sense one with the universe, the soul will ascend to him after death. All these ideas have no proof; they owe their formulation only to the poet's own consciousness. So, in 'The Prayer', the image of nature offering a hymn of praise to God in the temple of the universe at the altar of earth is crowned by a lone voice raised—the poet's:

> *Tout se tait: mon coeur seul parle dans ce silence.*
> *La voix de l'univers, c'est mon intelligence.*

[Everything is silent: only my heart speaks in this silence. The voice of the universe is my intelligence.]

This instinctive intelligence formulates and communicates its vision of God in images: He is outside all sensory experience, outside time and space, contained only in images of light and water. To Him the soul, freed from the impure weight of matter, will soar on bird-like wings. In the meantime—as for Gerard Manley Hopkins—it is the presence of God in nature which can give hope and comfort to man on earth. 'Hidden God ... nature is your temple' ('Immortality') is a frequent theme, leading to passages of entirely pantheistic verse. Indeed, in 'The Prayer', when Lamartine apostrophises God as soul of the universe, God, father, creator and Lord, he seems to admit indifference to the problem of what sort of belief he holds, for 'soul of the universe' is a stoic and pantheist concept, 'father' the Christian term, 'creator' the deist notion, and 'God' does duty for them all.

Lamartine himself maintained that his was essentially a Christian view, not only in the *Méditations* but also in *Jocelyn* and *La Chute d'un ange*, the two fragments of an unwritten epic which was to have been a kind of *Paradise Regained*. The general line of the work was to be the story of an angel who, falling in love with a mortal woman, is condemned to become a man, and only to find his way back to heaven after a series of purifying existences. This catalogue of expiations was to act as a symbol of humanity after the Fall, gradually ascending again towards the divine light. Of the two episodes actually written, *La Chute d'un ange* contains in its eighth 'vision' an account of how the fallen angel and his beloved flee to an inaccessible mountain, where a hermit, who guards a sacred book bearing precious little resemblance to the Bible, expounds to them a form of religion from which both cult and supernatural seem to have been excluded. *Jocelyn* is a less extravagant work, but although its theme is redemption by sacrifice— Jocelyn setting aside his love for Laurence to fulfil his duties as a priest—it is again a work from which Christ, and even God, are peculiarly absent. Religious fervour is conveyed not through the 'thought' of which Lamartine speaks so proudly in the Foreword —still less through the illogical brand of Christian rationalism he proposes in the Foreword to the seventh edition of *La Chute d'un ange*—but through the portrayal of states of ecstasy, such as that in the 'Second period' of *Jocelyn*, where the young hero offers up his soul to God in the darkened church. Sunset, the shadows, the sense of time past, the fabric of the cathedral as a symbol of the depth, mystery and eternity of God, the sense that the whole edifice is a sounding-board for celestial music, all these hold the reader's imagination as the verse sweeps up in a crescendo to the moment at which Jocelyn hears the voice of God itself:

> *L'âme éprouve un instant ce qu'éprouve notre oeil*
> *Quand, plongeant sur les bords des mers près d'un écueil*
> *Il s'essaie à compter les lames dont l'écume*
> *Etincelle au soleil, croule, jaillit et fume,*
> *Et qu'aveuglé d'éclairs et de bouillonnement*
> *Il ne voit plus que flots, lumière et mouvement*
> . . .
> *Et puis ce bruit s'apaise, et l'âme qui s'endort*
> *Nage dans l'infini sans aile, sans effort,*
> *Sans soutenir son vol sur aucune pensée,*
> *Mais immobile et morte et vaguement bercée.*

[The soul experiences for a moment what our eye experiences when, plunging onto the seashore close to a reef, it tries to count the billows whose foam sparkles in the sun, falls away, spurts up and steams, and when blinded by flashes of light and bubbling it can no longer see anything other than waves, light and movement . . . And then the sound grows quiet, and the sleeping soul floats wingless and effortless in the infinite, without supporting its flight on any thought, but motionless and dead and vaguely rocked.]

For Lamartine, whatever his protestations, religion is a totally emotional experience, detached from any coherent dogmatic or even philosophical basis. If it is not unkind to quote his line out of context, it could well be said that his religious poetry 'floats wingless and effortless in the infinite, without supporting its flight on any thought'.

It was not, however, merely an instinctive sense of respectability that made Lamartine protest his adherence to the official religion. Public opinion at its most educated level showed every sign of moving in his direction. Certainly by the 1830s official philosophy, in the persons of the eclectics Victor Cousin and Théodore Jouffroy, was expressing an attitude to religion that contains much of what was to be found in Chateaubriand and Lamartine. Cousin's cry to unite art, religion and fatherland harks back to some of Mme de Staël's claims in *De l'Allemagne* and to the underlying beliefs of *Le Génie du Christianisme*. And for Cousin, as with Lamartine, it is the instinctive self in the thinker who is given the exclusive voice in the formulation of truths about the universe, since 'spontaneous apperception' is seen as a prime factor in all consciousness. Via a complex and dubious concept of impersonal reason, what the self intuits is raised to an awareness of objective realities contained in what lies outside the self. These two worlds, the self and the non-self, correlative and reciprocally finite, must then be given an absolute and self-sufficient cause, namely God. God, as absolute cause, is absolute substance. His essence lies in his power to create, and he creates necessarily but spontaneously. He is not a pantheistic deity, since he is distinct from his creation, but neither is he a metaphysical abstraction, like the God of the deists. Man's relation to him is entirely through, again, his intuition. Established religion can be explained and defended as the systematisation by man of his initial perception of God into a system of symbols. 'The triumph of religious intuition lies in the creation of the forms of worship, just as the triumph of the idea of beauty lies in the creation of art.' The official philosophy of the day can be seen as adopting an essentially poetic attitude to religion while maintaining a respectful attitude to the established faith. If hocus-pocus of this sort passed for grave reasoning among the professional 'thinkers' of the land, it was hardly surprising if the metaphysics of poets was less than coherent.

From Lamartine via Cousin it is but a step to the religious views of Victor Hugo, for orthodox Christianity need no longer be accounted an integral element in the spiritual currents of the period. All three men were charged with pantheism; it is easy to see why. The charge is the most well-founded in relation to Hugo; yet, paradoxically, in some of his best known poems, such as 'Booz Asleep' from *La Légende des siècles*, he is the most Biblical of the three writers. It is not possible to find a coherent religious philosophy in Hugo's writings, any more than in Lamartine's, though in Hugo's case, in addition to the incoherence arising from the emotional basis of his beliefs, there is the fact that his creative lifespan was so long that his views were subject to understandable modifications of position on many major issues. None the less, works as diverse as his greatest novel, *Les Misérables*, and the epic cycle *La Légende des siècles* are very much concerned to show the place of transcendental values in the material world. Jean Valjean, the hero of *Les Misérables*, is a parable of man's fall and spiritual redemption, designed to show the enemies of the ideal of the 1848 Revolution that the belief in God and the immortality of the soul has civil liberty, progress and democracy as its corollary, and at the same time to convince the revolutionary party that materialism and atheism cannot produce a morality to satisfy the aspirations of the human heart. Here Hugo is working through pictures of the social life of France in his day—pictures admittedly as stylised and exaggerated as are some of Dickens's— but none the less conveying an emotive truth. In *Les Contemplations* Hugo uses the same spiritual position on a more individual plane, the different poems compounding the progress of a single soul. Of all these poems it is 'What the mouth of shadow says' that is the most revealing. The spirit offers man, who, in his blindness, refuses to recognise that there is anything in the universe that his own thought cannot encompass, a vision of creation as an endless ladder towards perfection (ie God), a ladder which also stretches down below man. It is death that reveals which way a man has moved on the ladder during his life. God is not, for Hugo, a Christian God who judges us. We create matter in our-

selves by our evil, and so descend the ladder. Or we lighten ourselves of matter by our good, and so ascend. Man is 'a prison in
which the soul remains free', free to choose the upward or the
downward path, but blind to this essential truth:

> Tes sages, tes penseurs ont essayé de voir;
> Qu'ont-ils vu? qu'ont-ils fait? qu'ont-ils dit, ces fils d'Eve?
> Rien . . .

[Your sages, your thinkers have tried to see; what have they seen?
what have they done? what have they said, these sons of Eve?
Nothing . . .]

Not all the poems are as abstract as this quotation suggests,
for Hugo believes in the affective example as the most compulsive
form of argument. In 'Something Seen One Spring Day' (*Contemplations*), for instance, the spiritual corruption of man is portrayed
through the emotive picture of the pathos of four hungry children
at their mother's bedside and the indifference of a materialistic
society to their plight. In another poem of the same collection—
'Mugitusque boum'— a different vein of emotional response is
tapped by a Wordsworthian appeal to nature; the message of
spiritual hope is detected by the attentive poet in the physical
world around him. This search for an effective image is codified in
La Légende des siècles into a cycle of pictures drawn from man's
history, starting with Biblical traditions and extending propheti-
cally into the future. What *Les Contemplations* does for the journey
of the individual soul is now attempted for humanity as a group:
the portrayal of the fall from paradise and then the slow ascent
towards the light. In his preface to the first series of the *Légende*,
Hugo calls it 'man's gradual unfolding over the centuries as he
climbs from darkness to the ideal, the transfiguration of the earthly
hell into paradise, the slow blossoming of the ultimate value—
freedom, justice for this life, responsibility for the next'. In the
final poem of the cycle, 'Abyss', each entity in turn, man, earth,
etc, rises via the stars to infinity, to hymn its own greatness. But

the last word, like the supreme power, lies with God: 'Je n'aurais qu' à souffler et tout serait de l'ombre' [one breath, and all would be darkness].

For Hugo, then, there is a God; he concerns himself with mankind, but he is unknowable. Our contact with him is intuitive and instinctive, as when, in *Les Misérables*, Monseigneur Bienvenu in his garden achieves contact with God in periods of silence, as he gazes at the stars. At the same time the human self, which is immortal and survives death, is responsible to God, who created it, and free to choose its own ascent or descent on the ladder of perfection. Religion has here moved far away from Christian orthodoxy. Indeed, Hugo is very scornful of the Church as an establishment and, like Voltaire, contrasts the figure of Christ as a symbol of man's innate goodness with the figure of the priest as embodiment of man's evil ('First Meeting of Christ with the Tomb' in *La Légende des siècles*). What is important for Hugo is the sense of the numinous, not properly pantheistic since God is still in some undefined way separate from his creation (cf the doctrine of Cousin), but close to pantheism. It is a religious sensibility presented as basic to man's moral development, and compatible with the revolutionary social attempt to improve the material conditions of the common man.

With Hugo, the question of metaphysical forces and their influence on mankind becomes intimately linked with problems of social morality, itself indivisible from the problem of individual morality. The triangular relationship between individual, society and cosmos is probably one of the most important literary themes of the early nineteenth century in France. Just as reason seemed insufficient as a moral sanction for society in general, so the power to exert rational control over one's own character development was suspect. Where a writer professed to understand man, it was now in terms of the dominant role played by the irrational in his motivation. 'All is hidden, all is unknown in the universe. Is not man himself a strange mystery?' Chateaubriand asked. One approach is simply to ignore the metaphysical aspect as insoluble, and concentrate on salvaging what pleasure one can from the irrational self. Stendhal, for example, bases his theory of human motivation on the idea that 'The body and head are servants of the soul, and the soul itself obeys the self, which is desire for happiness'—life only gains a meaning from passion expended in the pursuit of individual happiness. Other writers cling to the responsibility of external forces for the functioning of the inner man. The heroes of romantic drama are all portrayed as in the grip of powers that they cannot identify. Hugo's Hernani, from the play of the same name, defines himself thus:

> ... *Je suis une force qui va!*
> *Agent aveugle et sourd de mystères funèbres!*
> *Une âme de malheur faite avec des ténèbres!*
> *Où vais-je? je ne sais. Mais je me sens poussé*
> *D'un souffle impétueux, d'un destin insensé.*

[I am a moving force, a blind and deaf agent of fatal mysteries, a soul of misfortune, made of darkness. Where am I going? I do not know. But I feel myself impelled by an impetuous gust, by an insensate destiny.]

In either case an opposition is set up between those aware of man's predicament, and the ordinary man who, in Hernani's words, 'goes straight to the goal he has dreamed of'. Blindness, the blindness of the ordinary man to the mysteries of creation, both within him and without, condemns the intellectual to an élitist position —condemns or rewards, according to individual taste. Stendhal dedicates *La Chartreuse de Parme* to the 'happy few'. Hugo sees himself as Prometheus upon his rock, suffering that he may bring the torch of enlightenment to his fellows. But whether or not a writer considered all men capable of the status of hero-seer, they were all agreed that in their unwillingness to accept the truth, the common herd was a positive obstacle to the progress and happiness of the élite.

ALIENATED HERO AND HOSTILE SOCIETY

Only a gifted few could perceive the truth of the inadequacy of material surfaces, and those few could not agree on what lay beyond. The rest of society formed a body hostile to the aspirations of the individual for this life and (where applicable) for the next. Writers, therefore, had to choose between the portrayal of the world as it should be, in which the ideal could be realised, or the world as it was, in which reality provided a substantial, indeed an insuperable, barrier to the attainment of that ideal. To understand the effect of this on literature one should look first at the common characteristics of the various heroes, then at how they relate to their fellow men. The idea that the comprehension of the external world and the establishment of true values were dependent upon the exploration and comprehension of the needs and possibilities of the inner self received its literary expression either in figures representing a projection of the attainment of self-comprehension or in figures undergoing the difficult process of self-exploration. The eponymous hero of Chateaubriand's *René*, dimly aware of his insufficiencies but incapable of self-analysis, represents man at the beginning of the process; at the end of it, Alfred de Musset's Lorenzo (*Lorenzaccio*) or Stendhal's Julien Sorel (*Le Rouge et le Noir*) both ultimately achieve a form of self-knowledge, though for the former it represents failure and for the latter success of a peculiarly limited kind. For the ideal man, perfectly at harmony with his inner self through instinctive self-knowledge, one has to go either to the unreflecting Ivanhoe figures of the historical novel (*The Three Musketeers*, *The Queen's Necklace* and the rest of the vast production of Alexandre Dumas the elder) or, within a realistic framework, to figures of the poor and of children. Hugo's Jean Valjean (*Les Misérables*) achieves his final sanctification in extreme poverty, his grave symbolically returning to an anonymous state of nature; whilst in the same novel a succession of children, notably the orphan Cosette, reveal an instinctive perfection of character similar to that of Dickens's Little Nell. The reason for this curious alliance of what might better be called the un-historical novel and the portraiture of poverty and childhood is not difficult to find. The reading public was the adult middle-class, cushioned from poverty by their stocks and shares and from children by a proliferation of domestic servants—both areas of experience were to them as remote and exotic as the Middle Ages or the reign of Louis XIV. To be ideal by instinct, it is clear, is a dream state well removed in time or place from the average experience of the nineteenth-century Frenchman.

What, then, are the qualities of the 'ordinary' hero, left to pursue the ideal through self-examination? The prime element of self-awareness is alienation and loneliness. René exclaims:

> Alas! I was alone, alone on the earth! A secret listlessness was taking over my body. The distaste for life which I had felt since childhood came back with renewed strength. Soon my heart could no longer provide my mind with food for thought, and I was only aware of my existence through a profound sense of *ennui*.

Benjamin Constant's Adolphe (*Adolphe*) describes himself as 'this heart alien to all the interests of the world, alone in the midst of man, and yet suffering from the isolation to which it is condemned'. Alfred de Vigny transposes this alienation very appropriately into the figure of the poet Chatterton (*Chatterton*), seen as isolated from society by the nature of his poetic gifts and his extreme sensitivity.

For René, Chatterton and, in a different way, Adolphe, this awareness of alienation is a paralysing factor. But the response can be quite the opposite. What can broadly be termed 'Byronic revolt' leads to a self-conscious pursuit of the very elements that increase the isolation. The negative sense of alienation is made a positive craving for liberty, an identification of happiness with such liberty. In general, however, the writers of the period, while flirting with Byronism, preferred to remain genteely on the side of convention, admiring but reproving: 'There can be no honour where there is not virtue', wrote Lamartine in his *Méditations*, addressing Byron as 'fallen child of a divine race'. The great Byronic figure of the age is Alfred de Musset's Rolla, in the long poem of the same name. Debauched and godless, Rolla too has to be redeemed by a last moment of true love for one of the typical 'ideal' characters of the Romantic period—an innocent girl forced into prostitution by poverty. And Musset himself, while professing metaphysical despair in *Rolla*, takes good care to regret it:

> *Je ne crois pas, ô Christ, à ta parole sainte:*
> *Je suis venu trop tard dans un monde trop vieux.*
> *D'un siècle sans espoir naît un siècle sans crainte;*
> *. . .*
> *Ta gloire est morte, ô Christ, et sur nos croix d'ébène*
> *Ton cadavre céleste en poussière est tombé.*
> *En bien, qu'il soit permis d'en baiser la poussière*
> *Au moins crédule enfant de ce siècle sans foi,*
> *Et de pleurer, ô Christ . . .*

[O Christ, I do not believe in your holy word; I was born too late into a world too old. A century without fear is the child of a century without hope . . . Your glory is dead, O Christ, and on our ebony crosses your body has fallen into dust. Well, may the least credulous child of an age without faith be permitted to kiss its dust, and to weep, O Christ.]

Perhaps more significant than Byronic revolt in any metaphysical sense is the determination to create a valid alternative world within this world, a determination that animates the heroes of Stendhal or, in a different sense, Honoré de Balzac's arch-villain Vautrin (*Illusions perdues*, *Splendeurs et Misères des courtisanes*, *Père Goriot*). Here again, failure and success mark out quite different types, well represented by Musset's Lorenzo and Stendhal's Julien Sorel, both of whom undergo significant modifications of self-awareness. Lorenzo's character is the focal point of *Lorenzaccio* in much the same way that Brutus is the dramatic centre of Shakespeare's *Julius Caesar*. The scene is Florence, in the winter of

1536–7, a city in a ferment of discontent against the misrule of its tyrant, Alexander dei Medici. Lorenzo, his cousin, whose blood-claim to the dukedom is stronger than Alexander's, prepares to assassinate the tyrant, carries out the deed, and comes to a violent end in the aftermath. This political event is principally the vehicle for a study of the complicated interplay of inner forces to which Lorenzo is subject. For he has been two people: the idealist wanting to purge the world of an evil power and the man who, to gain the confidence of Alexander, has led a life of violence and debauchery as vicious as the duke's. In the process this mask of vice has become inseparable from the ideals that prompted its assumption. Lorenzo has realised, by the climax of the play, that he is no longer innocent; the irreconcilable tension between good and evil *is* his 'self'. By the time he kills Alexander, the act is no longer politically significant, for he predicts that it will fail to give the necessary lead to republican forces, and events confirm his forecast. Ultimately, the murder is significant only to himself. The key scene is act III sc 3, which forms almost a third of the total play. Philippe Strozzi, the moral leader of the opposition to Alexander, confronts Lorenzo, who in turn explains himself and his dilemma. He paints the purity of his youth, the sudden inspiration to become a tyrant-slayer, the fixing of his attention upon his cousin, the need to become acceptable to his cousin by adopting the semblance of Alexander's own iniquity:

> To please my cousin I had to reach him, carried forward by the tears of his victims' families; to become his friend and gain his confidence, I had to kiss all the crumbs of his orgies on his thick lips. I was pure as a lily, and yet I did not draw back before this task. Let us not talk of what I have become because of it. You must understand what I have suffered. There are wounds whose dressing one does not remove with impunity.

More than just corrupting himself, Lorenzo has learnt to the full the corruption of his fellow men, and it is this knowledge which has helped fix his own condition:

> The hand that has raised the veil of truth cannot let it fall again, it remains motionless until death, still holding the terrible veil and raising it higher and higher above men's heads, until the angel of sleep closes one's eyes for ever.

For Lorenzo the killing of his cousin has become the only way to retain contact with his old identity, to prevent the man from becoming totally the mask. The scenes of action which surround this central self-analysis serve to underline the duality within Lorenzo. But the duality is paradoxically shattered by the murder itself, for, by that action, Lorenzo deprives himself of his reason for existing. 'I was a machine built for murder, but for one murder alone.' His life has now only a hollow at its centre, and his death at the hands of an assassin leaves the world as if he has never been. He is a tragic hero not in the classical sense of a man struggling against external destiny. He creates his own destiny and destroys himself in the act. He has, in a sense, achieved his ideal of liberty, but it is irreconcilable with the realities of his fellow men and with his own need to be part of their society.

What Musset projects into the stylised form of historical drama, Stendhal incorporates into the more ambiguous domain of contemporary chronicle in *Le Rouge et le Noir*. Whereas Lorenzo realises in mid-stream that his self-creation has got out of hand, Julien Sorel is convinced until close to the end of his career that he really is master of his own destiny. Stendhal's concept of the 'chasse au bonheur', in which the individual's only possible course of action is the pursuit of satisfaction for his own passions, is not far removed from Lorenzo's reduction of political idealism to self-fulfilment. But Julien is shown undergoing the process of self-knowledge in a peculiarly complex way. He is aware that he possesses a fund of natural energy whose means of expression are minimal in the rigid and static society of the Restoration era (and, indeed, of the reign of Louis-Philippe for, in subtitling his novel 'Chronicle of 1830', whilst omitting any reference to the July Revolution, Stendhal deliberately suggests that nothing fundamental has changed in French society). He seeks to exploit that energy for social advancement, modelling himself on other examples of liberated self-expressors, of whom the first and greatest is Napoleon. Slowly he moves upward through a series of worlds—the provincial life of Verrières, the seminary at Besançon, the noble household of the de la Môles in Paris—only to find eventually that his moment of truth comes in the symbolic solitariness of prison. Admittedly he achieves his desired social advancement and the sexual conquests that attend upon it, but he achieves it in spite of the roles he forces himself to play. His campaign to seduce Mme de Rênal, mother of the children to whom he is tutor, fails; and he owes the actual seduction to the maternal compassion he arouses in her by bursting into tears over his failure. In Paris the reason why his employer's daughter, Mathilde de la Môle, falls in love with him is precisely that he is warily keeping her at a distance. At the seminary he attempts to win a place in his superior's esteem by intellectual superiority, but the only result is that he is suspected of spiritual pride. He parades his difference from the levels of society through which he ascends as a social difference and does not recognise that what he regards as his own greatest failing, his sensibility, is in fact the very secret of his superiority. For, throughout the novel, there are hints that if he could set aside the drive for social success and the obsession with casting himself in the mould of others, he has a very special emotional power. So, for example, we find him with Mme de Rênal and her friend Mme Derville, sitting in the evening cool under a spreading lime tree:

> Julien was no longer thinking of his dark ambitions, nor of those projects of his which would be so difficult to carry out. For the first time in his life he was carried away by the power of beauty. Lost in a vague, sweet day-dream, so unlike his usual character, as he gently squeezed the hand which he liked for its perfect prettiness, he was half-listening to the rustling of the leaves of the lime tree as the light night breeze ruffled them, and to the dogs of the Doubs mill as they barked in the distance.

It is the Julien who can respond in this way to nature, however rarely he does it, who will triumph. But, first, the search for social success, and its accidental attainment, force Julien into a more and more conventional mode until, when he achieves the status of officer and gentleman, the red coat which had been his goal as the symbol of energy and liberty has become the blue uniform of restraint and conformity. At this point, with one final flourish of energy, the true self finally reasserts itself. Mme de Rênal's letter to the Marquis de la Môle, revealing Julien's conduct towards her and thus attempting to prevent his forthcoming marriage with Mathilde, is the catalyst in releasing the true individuality of the hero. The great critical controversy over the highly and deliberately ambiguous way in which Stendhal presents Julien's attempt to shoot his former mistress is almost an irrelevance, for the significant thing is that Julien's wild act releases him from the strait-jacket of false success, leaving him free, in prison, to realise the true passion for Mme de Rênal which underlay his former hypocritical relationship with her. The core of the book's meaning lies in Julien's meditations before and after the trial, and in the act of suicide which his socially provocative speech to the jury constitutes. For, if there is a peculiarity about Julien's ultimate success, his realisation of his real 'self', it is that it looks suspiciously like ultimate failure to the unsympathetic reader. Mme de Rênal throws social convention to the winds and visits Julien in his cell; suddenly he acknowledges to himself and to her the fact that his love for her has been the only genuine achievement of his life. But this realisation is played against the backcloth of imminent death: Julien's by execution, Mme de Rênal's from grief. Their love is only possible when isolated from the social reality outside, as all achievement in Stendhal's novels turns out to be (hence the repetition of symbolic towers—places that shut in the hero and out the world). The hero can create his own valid world, but he cannot keep it alive in the face of the world outside himself.

It is this problem, the relationship of the élite hero to contemporary society, that provides the most interesting explorations of the theme of alienation. Not all the works that treat the theme are novels. Dumas the elder's play, *Antony*, attempts to tackle illegitimacy and adulterous love in the context of the upper-class drawing-room, but the breathless rhetoric of the hero sits ill with the social realism of the setting. Victor Hugo's social poetry, of which the alienated hero is the poet himself, deplores the blindness and insensitivity of his contemporaries in general and, in *Les Châtiments*, of Louis Napoleon in particular. Again the rhetoric is a barrier between the text and the modern reader. But, it was to be the novel which gave the widest scope for different interpretations of the clash of ideal and reality, and whether it could or should be resolved. Let us look at a group of representative works: Hugo's *Les Misérables*, Stendhal's *La Chartreuse de Parme*, Flaubert's *Madame Bovary* and *Education sentimentale* and Fromentin's *Dominique*.

Les Misérables is an epic denunciation of just about everything that Hugo considered rotten in the state of France, but it centres on the particular spiritual journey of Jean Valjean, condemned to the chain-gangs in his youth for stealing a loaf of bread, piling up extra prison sentence by his determined efforts to escape, and finding on his liberation that society has no pity or justice for the ex-convict. 'Liberation is not deliverance. One leaves the cell, but not the sentence.' Society has reduced Jean to such depths that the first person to show him kindness, Monseigneur Bienvenu, the elderly bishop, is rewarded by Jean stealing his silver cutlery. The bishop, by informing the gendarmes, who have picked up the wretched ex-convict 'on suspicion', that the silver was a gift, and by adding to it the pair of silver candelabra, instils in Jean the first feeling that he has the strength and duty to overcome the pressures of society in the name of an ideal good:

> The policemen departed. Jean Valjean was like a man on the point of fainting. The bishop approached him, and said in a low voice:

'Do not forget, do not ever forget, that you have promised to use this silver to become an honest man.'

Jean Valjean, who had no memory of promising anything at all, was tongue-tied. The bishop had stressed these words as he delivered them. He went on with a kind of solemnity: 'Jean Valjean, my brother, you are no longer in the hands of evil, but of good. I have bought your soul from you. I am disengaging it from the clutches of dark thoughts and from the spirit of perdition, and I am presenting it to God.'

That this redemption is no easy process is clear immediately from the following chapter, in which Jean meanly steals a coin from a poor child and is unable to persuade himself to give it back. But, as the novel unfolds and Jean's fate becomes entwined with that of other victims of the social system weaker than himself, he undergoes a consistent rise in moral stature. Established as the rich and benevolent industrialist M. Madeleine, he sacrifices everything, though after a hallucinatory scene of racking inner doubt, to prevent another convict, wrongly identified as Jean Valjean, from conviction for petty theft. Escaping from the clutches of the police, he devotes the rest of his life to bringing up an orphan girl, Cosette, amid the uncertainties of a Paris caught up in political turmoil. Despite the obsessive pursuit of the determined policeman, Javert, symbol of blinkered duty, he lives to see Cosette financially established and married, and dies in what can only be called an odour of sanctity, having raised himself on the ladder of being, one supposes, by his superhuman will to goodness.

'My children, I can no longer see quite clearly. I still had things to say to you, but never mind. Think of me a little. You are blessed creatures. I do not know what is the matter with me, I can see light, Come a little closer. I am dying happy. Give me your dear, beloved heads so that I can rest my hands on them.'

Cosette and Marius fell on their knees, overcome, choking with tears, each taking one of the hands of Jean Valjean. Those august hands were still. He had fallen back, the light of the two candlesticks fell on him: his pale face was looking up to heaven. He let Cosette and Marius cover his hands in kisses. He was dead.

The night was starless and profoundly dark. Doubtless up there in the shadow some vast angel was standing, his wings outstretched, waiting to receive the soul.

The story is immensely sentimental, but powerful in its visionary qualities, with character after character achieving symbolic status against a backdrop of France, particularly Paris, in which the description of living conditions and social conduct is intensified by the sheer piling of horror upon horror. Hugo certainly communicates very vividly the hopelessness of utter poverty, and the reasons for rejecting the system that makes it possible. But, when he comes to the picture of the qualities necessary if a man is to win through against the overwhelming odds, the result is a hero in whom only an idealist can believe. The result of projecting, as the sole effective combatant against material evil, a never-never knight in shining armour, which is what Jean Valjean becomes once incarnated as M Madeleine, is profoundly depressing. 'Jean Valjeans', we feel, do not exist; starving children, blinkered policemen, innocent people dying for hopeless causes did exist, and still do.

A very different and much more ambiguous juxtaposition of élite hero and hostile society is to be found in the novels of Stendhal. *La Chartreuse de Parme* is at first sight slightly out of place in the company of novels such as *Les Misérables* and *Education sentimentale*, for its setting is the exotic world of nineteenth-century Italy, with its proliferating petty princedoms and endless sterile intrigues. Moreover, the nineteenth-century element is overlaid with a stylised picture of the brasher and more violent Italy of the late Renaissance, as Zola first observed in his article 'Naturalist Novelists':

> I confess that I find it extremely difficult to accept Stendhal's Italy as the Italy of the contemporary period. He seems to me to have depicted fifteenth-century Italy, with its large-scale poisonings, its

sword-play, its spies and masked bandits, its extraordinary adventures in which love bloomed and thrived amid a welter of bloodshed.

However, the hero of the novel, Fabrice del Dongo, is, despite the Renaissance patina of his surroundings, essentially a contemporary figure, in that he is looking for a meaning to his life in a society which is content with rigidified formulae as a substitute for action, thought and feeling. It is interesting in this respect to compare him with Julien Sorel and with Lucien Leuwen, the eponymous hero of Stendhal's substantial but unfinished novel of political life under the Second Empire. Julien is the only one of these three heroes who is concerned with social mobility, for Lucien and Fabrice are born at the top already. But each discovers that society is a stultifying place—and the three novels taken together clearly show that Stendhal moves from denouncing specific societies, the France of the Bourbon Restoration (1815–30), and that of Louis-Philippe, to denouncing the mechanisms of society in general, under the guise of the courts of Ernest-Ranuce IV and V. For Stendhal, only in the unique passions of the heart can the self-aware man find fulfilment; here, too, society interposes its veto. Julien's Mme de Rênal, Lucien's Mme de Chasteller, Fabrice's Clélia are all women whom barriers of previous marriage, coupled with class differences or political allegiances, place beyond the hero's legitimate attainment. It is only in those classic symbols of isolation and superiority—Julien's prison and the Farnese tower in which Fabrice is incarcerated—that the idyll of true passion can be attained. When Fabrice and Clélia attempt to carry on a secret affair in the 'real' world, it leads, however unmelodramatically, to the death of both of them. *Amour-passion*, it would seem, can only be sustained in a vacuum.

It is not clear, however, to what extent this is actually the fault of society. In *Le Rouge et le Noir*, the pretensions of the *nouveau-riche* circle of Verrières and the atrophy of *bien-pensant* royalist circles in Paris are undoubtedly a cause of the gradual stifling, and hence misdirection, of Julien's natural energies. It is difficult to see whether either Lucien or Fabrice really possesses any such driving force to begin with. Even in Julien's case it is true that the decisive steps are always taken for him by someone else: his father and M de Rênal between them settle his first job, as tutor; the Abbé Chêlan gets him into the seminary; Pirard arranges for him to leave there and enter the service of M de la Môle as secretary. Yet at least he has earned their assistance by his personal qualities, if not exactly by his merits. In contrast, Lucien is precipitated into his changes of occupation by the spur of mere vanity. He enters the army because his cousin chides him for living at his father's expense, the absurd miscarriage of his love affair in Nancy precipitates him back on Paris; there, by his father's manoeuvring, he is duly retired from the army and enters government service. It is in fact his father's death and the absence of the expected inheritance which liberate Lucien. Whereas Lucien seems controlled by his internal impulses and released from them by an external agency, Fabrice never appears to achieve full release at all. He is a passive tool in the hands of his vivacious aunt Gina and the well-tried politician Count Mosca, until such time as chance throws him into contact with Clélia Conti in the prison where her father is governor.

Such adventures as Fabrice undertakes off his own bat turn out absurdly, as with his participation in the battle of Waterloo, or precipitate disasters upon himself and those around him, as in the adventure with the actress whose lover, Giletti, he is forced to kill in self-defence. Julien may mislead himself by over-analysis and by fitting his life to alien patterns. Fabrice, with Stendhal's approval, is incapable of thought at all. He has been taught by his Jesuit teachers that self-examination is a sin, a 'step towards Protestantism'. Accordingly, he never questions his own existence and has no consistent image of himself to which he is attempting to live up. At the most he questions in a naïve rhetorical way quite what is taking place around and to himself, whether the situation

37

be love or war. He accepts as a matter of course a career in the Church and his future as archbishop of Parma, arranged for him by Gina and Mosca; he is not particularly disturbed when the Giletti affair puts an end to that career. He is, in fact, merely an indulgent hedonist whose conversion to a tragic figure is executed abruptly under the *coup-de-foudre* of love. If society is villain in *La Chartreuse de Parme*, it is because the political alignment of that conservative liberal, Clélia's father, Fabio Conti, against that liberal conservative, Fabrice's aunt, prevents the natural union of the two young people. In all other respects the life of Fabrice is so frivolous that it is difficult not to regard him as the silliest hero created by any nineteenth-century novelist. This impression is heightened if Fabrice is set against the mature characters, Gina and Mosca. Gina has been genuinely forced by social restrictions to modify herself, firstly because her natural sympathy for the values represented by the Napoleonic cause is out of joint with the political conditions of post-Waterloo Europe, and secondly because the love she conceives for her nephew is outside the bounds permitted by convention. Mosca has shackled himself by submitting to the rules of the political games which are a substitute for significant power in an absolutist world. These two characters are no less engaged in the pursuit of happiness than Fabrice, but they have minds, emotions, obligations that make them infinitely more sympathetic.

Stendhal's vision of the élite self and its survival in a mediocre world is one in which instinct or, to be more precise, passion is given its head, and the ensuing pursuit of self-satisfaction, though it does not withstand the pressures of reality, gives a temporary meaning to existence. Temporary, because Julien is executed, Fabrice, Clélia and even their sad little illicit baby, Sandrino, die, and Stendhal abandons *Lucien Leuwen* at a point where he seems unable to bring Lucien and Mme de Chasteller together without destroying the story's credibility. The idylls of Julien and Mme de Rênal, or of Fabrice and Clélia, may be touching, but they do not seem to add up to much as the culmination of a whole life's endeavours, particularly when placed in the context of so selfless a visionary work as *Les Misérables*. At the same time, Stendhal's novels seem less than realistic if compared with the ruthless exposition of the would-be élite dreamers at the centre of Gustave Flaubert's two major works, *Madame Bovary* and *Education sentimentale*.

Emma Bovary and her counterpart, Frédéric Moreau, have both been brought up on a diet of literature in which the superior qualities of heroes and heroines transport them into a realm of social, artistic and emotional achievement beyond the grasp of ordinary mortals. Emma from her schooldays has been a great devourer of romantic novels:

> It was all love affairs, lovers, beloveds, importuned ladies swoon-ing behind isolated summer-houses, postillions who get killed at every posting-house, horses ridden into the ground on every page, dark forests, trembling hearts, oaths, sobs, tears, kisses, skiffs on moonlit waters, nightingales in the thickets, men as brave as lions, as gentle as lambs, more virtuous than anyone ever could be, always beautifully dressed, and weeping buckets of tears. At the age of sixteen, for six months, Emma soiled her hands with this fustian circulating-library stuff.

Her religious education includes passages from Chateaubriand's *Génie du Christianisme*; her later reading introduced her to the cult of historic greatness and the picturesqueness of the historical novel *à la* Walter Scott. Even the lyrics of the music she learns in her singing classes contribute to her picture of a dream world beyond the banalities of her everyday life. The effect of all this is to encourage in Emma a belief in the possibility of living a life at a pitch of heightened sensibility that is as yet placed as far beyond her reach as the exotic America of Bernardin de Saint-Pierre's *Paul et Virginie* or the tapestry medievalism of *Ivanhoe*. None the less it has the serious result that Emma creates both a picture of her own potential self and a yard-stick for others which bear no relation to the way real people function. She sees marriage, for example, as an exciting and emotionally stimulating institution, endows Charles Bovary with the imaginary qualities of an ideal husband, and is then disappointed and bewildered by the actual experience of married life:

> Before she married, she had thought she was in love; but as the happiness that should have resulted from that love had not materialised, she must have been mistaken, she thought. And Emma wondered what exactly corresponded in life to the words felicity, passion and intoxication which she had found so beautiful in books.

The natural first step from this position is to assume that the fault lies not with her own vision but with Charles. Swiftly Emma moves to a position in which Charles can do no right, a view which some critics have taken as the reality. Yet when Emma criticises Charles for us, the false measure of the sentimental hero is always clearly visible in her thoughts:

> Charles' conversation was as flat as a pavement, and the ideas of the whole world were to be seen there in their everyday dress; they excited neither emotion, laughter or dream. In all the time he lived in Rouen he had never thought, he said, of going to see the Parisian company that toured at the theatre. He could not swim, fence or shoot, and he had failed, one day, to explain to her a riding term which she had come across in a novel. Should a man, on the contrary, not know everything? Should he not excel at many different activities? Should he not initiate you into the forces of passion, the refinements of life, all its mysteries?

No man could possibly fulfil the pattern of a husband proposed here, for it is simply an assembly of the trappings of a novelette hero, with no definable character qualities at all.

Crisis point for Emma is reached when she and Charles attend a ball at the local château. To the reader it is merely a routine affair, undertaken by the Marquis d'Andervilliers to drum up a little political support. But Emma is, as ever, blind to the facts.

Every detail is made to symbolise something far more beautiful until the whole event transports her into an exotic world akin to that of her dreams. When it is all over, the details gradually fade but there remains implanted in her firstly the conviction that a lifestyle compatible with her dreams exists, and secondly that what she lacks for the acquisition of that lifestyle is money. From the impossible worlds of the past or of distant lands her imagination becomes fixed on Paris. Her reading changes accordingly; she buys a map of Paris, she takes out subscriptions to women's magazines. From now until her death Emma relentlessly pursues the obsession that her dreams are translatable into material terms. She allows herself to be seduced by Rodolphe, an uxorious gentleman farmer who plays up to her fantasies for his own amusement, until such time as she begins to seem tiresome. Just as she has never understood the real Charles, so she never sees the real Rodolphe. He merely appears to conform to her concept of the perfect lover because it suits him to. Nor does she understand herself, but transfers herself into each new role according to the literary pattern she has assimilated:

> Then she remembered the heroines of the books she had read, and the massed choirs of those adulterous wives started to sing in her memory with sisterly voices which enchanted her. She herself was becoming, as it were, a real part of her imaginings, and carrying into effect the long dream of her youth, as she saw herself as the type of lover she had always envied.

Every step of her life is governed by illusion, down to the way that she treats her poor child, the elopement which she plans but Rodolphe never intends to carry out, the attitude which she takes to religion when she feels in spiritual need, her passing attempt to make Charles into a great doctor.

Her final love affair, with the young clerk Léon, gives her as a lover a character so plastic that she can almost mould him into the image she desires. It is interesting to see how, for one brief moment, she and Léon actually do achieve the kind of stylised bliss that

Emma is pursuing. They spend three days together in a hotel in Rouen 'with the shutters across, the doors closed, flowers scattered on the ground, and iced grenadine served to them first thing in the morning'. They take a trip in a covered boat to a little island, where, in a low-ceilinged restaurant, they dine on whitebait, and cherries and cream. Then they row back in their covered boat by moonlight, with Emma singing that classic poem of nostalgia, Lamartine's 'The Lake'. All the images are designed to show their careful exclusion of the real world, the insubstantiality of their life style, the fragility of the carefully engineered experience. Indeed, so fragile is it that the boatman inadvertently shatters the effect by bringing up a reference to Rodolphe.

What Emma betrays in her frantic effort to associate dream with reality is not only her self-deception but also the mediocrity of the values with which she is seeking to replace reality. In two famous set-pieces Flaubert cruelly underlines the way Emma thinks and expresses herself in clichés every jot as banal as those that encapsulate the everyday life of the little Normandy community in which she lives. The first of these scenes takes place in the inn at Yonville, on Charles' and Emma's arrival in the village. In the background we hear the clack of the servants' shoes on the tiles of the floor; in the middle-ground the pretentious apothecary Homais discourses to Charles about the geographical and meteorological situation of the town, and in the foreground Emma and the would-be aesthete Léon are exchanging sensibilities on nature, music and literature. Each level of sound acts as a comment on the others, the words being reduced to the value of empty voices. The second such scene, at the agricultural show, is an extended and even more carefully orchestrated example of the same technique. This time the picture is vertical, the ordinary people and animal pens at ground level, the local worthies on the platform, and Rodolphe and Emma watching the prize-giving from a first-floor window of the town hall. Political rhetoric and love rhetoric alternate, neither being more meaningful than the sound of chairs scraping or the lowing and bellowing of the tethered animals. Flaubert exposes not only the inadequacy of what Emma (and her lovers) say, but also their failure to perceive things which in reality come close to the sort of beauty they purport to be seeking. So Emma and Rodolphe stroll through a moonlit landscape described by Flaubert with great skill as something magical; their response to it is utterly mundane, ' "Ah! What a fine night!" Rodolphe said. "We shall have others," Emma replied.' Rodolphe experiences only a superficial response to the night; Emma reduces it to part of a future sequence. True beauty in the present is beyond their comprehension.

When one sees her in this light, one is tempted to dismiss Emma as a rather silly woman who cannot come to terms with the responsibilities of everyday life. However, Flaubert makes it plain that the world around Emma really is as tiresome and narrow as she thinks it is, if for different reasons. The hypocrisy, platitudinousness, cowardice and pretensions of Homais and the insensitivity and spiritual inadequacy of the hard-working but dim Abbé Bournisien symbolise between them the basic range of shortcomings in the world of Yonville. In that sense it is a virtue of Emma to dream, but a virtue which, for Flaubert, is aborted, essentially, by the shortcomings not of her imagination but of the language in which it has to be clothed. In case we should fall into the trap of passing judgement, Flaubert at one point even steps out of his impersonal narrative to remind us of this fact. In part 2 chapter 12, Rodolphe has been listening to the effusions of Emma with growing impatience, finding her more and more like all his previous mistresses:

> He could not tell, experienced a man as he was, the dissimilarity of the feelings under the similarity of expression. Because libertine or bought lips had murmured similar phrases, he had little faith in the artlessness of these; she should cut down a bit, he thought, on the exaggerated speeches, given the mediocrity of the affection that they covered;

43

Without pause, Flaubert shows the narrowness of such a view:

> ... as if the fullness of the soul did not sometimes overflow in the emptiest of metaphors, since nobody could ever give the exact measure of his needs, or his conceptions, or his sorrows, for human speech is like a cracked pot on which we beat out tunes for bears to dance to when we are trying to touch the heart of the stars.

The value of what Emma, or anyone else, feels cannot be judged from the distortions placed on it by the conventions of language.

Emma Bovary lives in a world as unpromising in its way as that of Jean Valjean or Julien Sorel. But, like Julien, she expends her energies on attempting to mould reality to her own illusion. Unlike Julien she destroys herself in the process, and there is no moment of pure achievement to match his prison idyll. On the contrary, the supreme irony for Emma is that the pursuit of her illusion entangles her more and more in the messy realities of debt and financial disgrace, until it is these alone which trigger off her unpleasant and 'unheroic' suicide. When it is too late, she realises that Charles, for all his faults, did genuinely love her. Charles' reward is to die the romantic death by decline that would so well have befitted the Emma of her own vision.

Frédéric Moreau, the hero of *Education sentimentale*, and his childhood friend, Deslauriers, demonstrate the same view of the incompatibility of the world as it is with the élitist self's desire to live on some higher plane. Deslauriers at school reads books on metaphysics; Frédéric is fascinated with the Middle Ages. Frédéric's ambition is to become the Walter Scott of France; Deslauriers wants to create a vast system of philosophy with universal applications. The focus of the novel is on the pursuit and failure of Frédéric's dreams, but those of Deslauriers are always in the background, following the same rise and fall. Moreover, both young men are symbols of the rise and fall of the whole political and social ideal of the generation of 1848, which is itself a running theme of the action. What Flaubert does is to extend the study of the élite individual into a wider sphere. Emma had moved from the isolation of her father's farmhouse to the little village of Tostes, and on to the small town of Yonville, finding in each the same kind of spiritual claustrophobia. For her, escape seemed always across the hill, as it were, in Rouen, or in the Paris that she never visited. Frédéric is a native of Nogent—for Flaubert's purposes roughly the equivalent of Rouen. He moves outward into Paris, and eventually (part 3 chapter 6) into the whole world —only to discover that spiritual claustrophobia exists everywhere. Emma tries to mould physical reality to her own dream-pattern by manipulating other people and her personal relations with them. Frédéric attempts the same thing in other areas of human experience, notably the arts and politics. Only in the field of love is Frédéric almost content to keep ideal and realisation apart, for he pursues the woman he 'loves', Mme Arnoux, with a feminine timidity in marked contrast to the masculine decisiveness of Emma. Frédéric, too, has no power to see himself as he really is— not that anyone else by definition has such a power either. But, unlike Emma, his perceptions of other people fluctuate. Sometimes, the triviality of the worlds of the courtesan, the small-time entrepreneur, the grand financier is all too apparent to him. As soon as his own ambitions are engaged, the patina of idealisation returns. Above all, his relationship with Mme Arnoux, because it is never consummated, remains almost to the end a dream untarnished. At a stage in his life when all other aspirations have long been abandoned, he meets Mme Arnoux again, and the merest hint that she might be ready to give herself to him, after all these years, is enough to shatter the fragile shell of his one remaining illusion. He thinks he has preserved it intact:

> Suddenly she pushed him away with an air of hopelessness; and, as he was begging her to say something to him, she bowed her head and said: 'I should have liked to make you happy.' Frédéric suspected Mme Arnoux of having come to give herself to him; and he was seized by a lust that was stronger than ever, mad insane. Yet he felt something indescribable, a revulsion, something like fear of incest.

Another fear held him back, that of feeling disgust afterwards. Moreover, what complications it would cause!—and from a mixture of prudence, and the desire not to degrade his ideal, he turned on his heels and began to roll a cigarette.

Yet, in fact, even this near-contact has been too much. Once an illusion is identified as an illusion, it loses its powers. With Mme Arnoux's departure, nothing is left. Years later still, the only merit which Frédéric and Deslauriers, whose political and personal life has also been a failure, can find in their past is the occasion when as boys they went to a brothel carrying bunches of flowers, and, losing their nerve, left before their expectations could be disappointed. Life, Flaubert seems to say, is a cheap and nasty whore; the innocent who comes to her bearing gifts of beauty will only survive by turning his back on her, for the experience will sour him ineradicably.

If Stendhal offers a world which appears to stifle the gifts of the would-be hero until he can somehow isolate himself and escape from it, Flaubert offers, in these two novels, a world which flatly excludes such achievement, where the dreamer is his own worst enemy and the 'pursuit of happiness' can only lead to physical or spiritual death. If there are any characters in Flaubert who have a capacity for true 'happiness', they are always, paradoxically, stupid and to a large degree unable to verbalise. The truest affections in *Madame Bovary* are those of Charles for Emma or of Justin, the apothecary's little assistant, who weeps silently over her grave. In *Education sentimentale* the most sympathetic figure is poor, dim Dussardier, believing intensely in his duties to his fellow workers, yet finding himself helping to suppress their uprising against the republican government. It is outside the two major novels, to the first of the *Trois contes*, 'A Simple Heart', that we must look for the extreme example of this phenomenon. Old Felicity, duped and exploited all her life yet entirely at peace with the world, is gradually deprived of contact with reality by the loss of those dear to her, then by the loss of her own faculties. Her life centres in the end on the stuffed parrot, which becomes confused with the image of the Holy Ghost as she has seen it in coloured illustrations at Church; as she dies, the parrot-spirit seems to be waiting to welcome her into paradise. The illusion, however much it *is* an illusion, has sufficed to bring her a type of happiness unknown to Emma and Frédéric. All of the *Trois contes* feature this same ambiguous religious ending, in which an isolated figure achieves a happiness that may be totally illusory (see pp. 116–20 for a broader discussion of this point). Each is, in his way, a fanatic and a person as devoid of the characteristics of the élite hero as one could possibly hope to find. It is as if Flaubert has stood the romantic world on its head and portrayed the goal of the idealist as only accessible to the least likely members of society.

Unique in its handling of how to reconcile the pursuit of ideals with the restrictions of reality is the sole novel of Eugène Fromentin, *Dominique* (1862), for it rejects both the isolationism of the Stendhalian solution and the despair of Flaubert. *Dominique* is the record of a quest, a mental journey back into childhood undertaken in order to describe the process of suffering which has culminated in the narrator's self-knowledge. That the narrator *has* achieved self-knowledge, and with it peace, is plain from the very opening of the book:

> I have found certainty and peace, which is worth more than any theory. I have come to terms with myself, which is the greatest victory we can win over the impossible ... So I have nothing to complain about. My life is fashioned, and well fashioned, according to my desires and merits.

It is a novel without a plot, in the conventional sense. At the beginning and end, the personality of Dominique is seen at rest, solidly anchored in the reality of family life. The central and greater part of the book traces the development and course of his love affair with his cousin, Madeleine, a love affair representing the search for individuality, for what divides one from the world. By eventually renouncing all claims to Madeleine, Dominique acquiesces in his re-integration into society; indeed, when Augustin, his intellectual *alter ego*, greets him in the closing words of the novel, it is with his patronymic, 'Hello, de Bray', symbolising Dominique's now established role as a member of the clan. Potentially, Dominique is another Frédéric Moreau, and his relationship with Madeleine, who marries another while Dominique is still too young to be considered a serious rival, follows the same pattern of hopeless pursuit and emotional torture as does Frédéric's of Marie Arnoux. But the narrating Dominique is now at a distance from all that. He can appreciate the subtle, almost imperceptible variations to which his adolescent character was subject. Above all he unearths the way in which his adolescent readiness for love crystallises around his cousin, such that the fact of loving is primary, the search for possession secondary. Madeleine's husband has no suspicions of Dominique, who comes to Paris simply to be near her; yet the lovers themselves find constant obstacles to prevent a consummation which—as Frédéric Moreau, too, senses—would devalue the ideal of love itself.

The power of Fromentin's characterisation depends very largely on his use of symbols. The cycle of the seasons is a sympathetic accompaniment to successive or recurrent psychological states. Awakening of sentiment and sexuality takes place in spring, disappointments and trials occur in winter, the elegiac repose of the beginning and end are set in autumn. In a similar way the sea acts as a permanent symbol of the presence of passion. Dominique can always hear it from his house, 'Les Trembles'; he takes a daily ride to the shore, but he has learnt to turn his back on it. For the adult, the romantic and dangerous elements are never far from the surface, but are under control. By contrast, at the most dangerous moment of their relationship Dominique and Madeleine actually go out on a boat trip. Perhaps the most far-reaching of these psychological symbols is the description of Dominique's study, which contains all the elements essential to his childhood, some of them, like the portrait, apparently totally disconnected from the adult figure, others suggesting a central reality which remains the same however it is modified. The study within the house is like the young Dominique within the old, something still essential to the whole, but tamed and made to play its proper restricted role. It is a very middle-aged solution, the calm acceptance of the *juste-milieu*, with just a tinge of idealism remaining in that Dominique is integrated into an isolated rural community and not into the mainstream of urban French life. Fromentin faces up to the fact that the idealist element cannot be eradicated from a man's character, but that, as Dickens suggests in *David Copperfield*, the attainment of happiness is strictly related to a realistic assessment of one's own limitations.

It is a long way from the emotional mysticism of *René* to the pragmatic materialism of the mature Dominique, but the urge to find, either beyond the bounds of material reality or within the special gifts of the élite self, some compensation for the inadequacy of the contemporary world is in essence the same kind of reaction to the same kind of stimulus. Yet it would be a mistake to suppose that all those who were dissatisfied with the status quo pursued their illusions on the highly individualist level of a Julien Sorel or an Emma Bovary. Nor were the transcendental intuitions of an Hugo the sole approach to social problems. Many writers and thinkers were concerned with maintaining the eighteenth-century scientific traditions. They, too, were not without their illusions.

CHAPTER 2

Science, Reason and the Material World

In early nineteenth-century France it was in the sciences themselves that the development of experimental method, the use of
reason and the search for material progress were principally
pursued. But as the major discoveries were made in the very area
of science which touched most nearly on man's concept of his
own nature—that is, in the biological sciences—it seemed a
relatively small step to move from the attitudes and methods of
Lamarck, whose *Natural History of Invertebrates* appeared between
1815 and 1822, and of Geoffroy Saint-Hilaire, whose *Anatomical
Philosophy* belongs to the same period (1818–22), to theories of the
nature and function of society which would establish the parallels
between man's kingdom and that of the animals. The attraction of
such parallels was that, given the evolutionary principles of the
new biology, such a connexion (or imagined connexion) would
provide a basis from which to promote social change.

Already in 1814 Saint-Simon had begun to propose, in his *On
the Reorganisation of European Society*, various rationalisations of
social structure, and his *On the Industrial System* (1821–2) expanded
the question to broader economic issues. Saint-Simon feared that

from the confusion of early nineteenth-century society there would arise an economic hierarchy as rigid as the old political one. In order to avoid this, he proposed a machinery of government organised on purely rational lines, with the responsibility for the management of society resting with those engaged in the arts, sciences and industry. But Saint-Simon's writings lacked scientific precision, and it was not entirely surprising that his followers turned his new social order from a reasoned theory into a utopian religion.

The first thinker of the period who can more properly be compared with Cuvier (the naturalist), Lamarck and the scientific tradition is Auguste Comte, in whom we also find the founder of what was to be the great positivist tradition that dominated French philosophy 1830–80. Comte, who had been Saint-Simon's secretary, was particularly struck by *Memorandum on the Application of Physiology to the Amelioration of Social Institutions*. In this work Saint-Simon had proposed the view of society as a collective organism, subject to a process of evolution such as the pre-Darwinian biologists had recently attributed to other living organisms. The study of the history of civilisation was accordingly to become the study of the history of the social organism as it developed its various 'organs'. From this idea Comte was to develop the famous 'law of the three estates' which is one of the fundamentals of his philosophical position. Comte's aim in developing his system was to reorganise society using intellectual reform as a basis. To reform institutions alone was to deal, he thought, only with the symptoms of social anarchy, the cause of which he located in the break-up of the cohesion of intellectual values consequent on the French Revolution. In contemporary society (ie, *c*1830) he detected the co-existence of three principal and incompatible intellectual systems, his 'three estates'. The first is theology, which attributes material phenomena to the will of God; the second is metaphysical philosophy, which replaces God by abstract principles that do not differ essentially in kind from the concept of a divine being; the third is positivism, the philosophical embodiment of scientific method, which confines itself to observing the laws governing material phenomena, and refuses the possibility of all transcendental explanations.

These three systems—theology, metaphysics and positivism—are proposed by Comte as representing the three stages of thought or intellectual growth potentially undergone by both any given individual and any given group of individuals—ie, by any society. He accordingly explains the chaotic state of contemporary values as being occasioned by the co-existence of individuals who have reached different stages of development. The solution would be firstly to impose the principle that positivism is the only acceptable developed form of thought, then to apply the general intellectual method of positivism to a science of society. This science, in essence an early concept of sociology, is proposed by Comte as summit to a hierarchy of sciences which, in partaking of the principles appertaining to all forms of knowledge, represents their *summa*.

For Comte, then, science and knowledge are interchangeable terms, and the function of the physical sciences is to offer patterns of cause and effect which can be applied to human behaviour. This is not a purely descriptive exercise. Comte rejects the observation of facts as an end in itself—ie, pure empiricism. Science for him must be a system of laws marking necessary and invariable relationships between phenomena. Reason is therefore the essential tool. On the basis of observed fact, hypotheses are to be formulated whose nature is merely that of anticipation of facts which experience and reason could have demonstrated, had the circumstances of the experiment been favourable. Over and above the processes of each individual science Comte then projects a philosophy of science which, by bringing together the laws of individual sciences, will deduce the universal scientific order—the 'law of laws'.

The most influential detailed exposition of the virtues of

scientific method came not from Comte, who was in too much of a hurry to attain his abstract conclusions to linger over the detail that was to contribute to them, but from a genuine scientist, Claude Bernard. Though Bernard was primarily interested in promoting the experimental development of medicine, and though he was sufficiently critical of philosophical speculation to say that 'the best philosophical system is to have none at all', none the less, his *Introduction to the Study of Experimental Medicine* (1865) was influential on circles well outside his own profession, not least upon Emile Zola's theoretical writings on the novel, *The Experimental Novel* (1880). The cause of this influence was precisely the fact that Bernard's work embodies a theory of knowledge, and one that is in essence positivist. He affirms that our only means of knowing reality is by the observation of phenomena, and by the deduction of general laws on the basis of that observation. Unlike Comte, he accepts that the knowledge which this method establishes will always be provisional and relative, since, though no fact may hitherto have been discovered to modify a particular scientific conclusion, the potential discovery of such a fact must always be allowed for. Reality, for him, is definable only in terms of a series of 'conditions' whose ultimate cause science cannot establish, but whose patterns it can describe, and thence predict the recurrence of similar patterns. This does not exclude the non-rational element in human existence. He roundly condemned those thinkers of his time who proscribed metaphysical questioning and religious feelings. For him, belief remained an essential part of the human condition. His objection to metaphysics and theology was that they purported to offer knowledge where in fact they offered only opinion on the unknowable.

To the modern reader Bernard seems to be harping on the obvious in his definition of scientific method, its uses and limitations. At the period in which he was writing, however, his own speciality was still far from properly experimental in its research, and in allied fields some scientists were still prepared to subordinate experimental evidence to Christian beliefs (Edmund Gosse's portrait of his biologist father in *Father and Son* is a case in point). More importantly, in the years that elapsed between Comte's *Course of Positivist Philosophy* and Bernard's *Experimental Medicine*, the name of science and the concept of reality had been invoked in two ways: scientism and dogmatic materialism, neither of which Bernard felt to be justified, and both of which he felt it his duty to combat. The promoters of scientism were those positivists who claimed that science could offer a new ethic, and bring about the perfecting of society. This, for Bernard, was to raise science to the status of a religion, and thus to step outside the field of genuine scientific method. However, those positivists who asserted that material phenomena as we experience them are the only reality, were equally adopting a position as dogmatic as any metaphysical creed. As Bernard put it, 'positivism which in the name of science rejects philosophical systems has, like them, the disadvantage of being a system'. The idealist element essential to scientism—and present, as we shall see, in the thought of the later major positivist thinkers, Ernest Renan and Hippolyte Taine—fits the philosophy into the same complicated network of tensions between aspiration and pragmatism that we have already observed in the work of Stendhal, Flaubert and Fromentin. But the aspect of positivism which endeared it to the France of Louis-Philippe and the Second Empire was the determined materialism that Bernard so disliked.

MATERIALISM AND THE THEATRE

Perhaps the area of literature in which a largely materialist approach gained the greatest hold was the theatre. A fairly thorough-going theory of dramatic realism—what Beaumarchais called 'the faithful portrayal of man's acts'—had been current in France well before the end of the eighteenth century, and from that period onward contemporary social problems made an increasingly large contribution to the *matter* of French plays. But the flowering of this type of drama in the 1840s and after has a commercial explanation. Dramatists are particularly exposed to the influence of public taste. Under the First Empire and in the early years of the Restoration, public taste—as opposed to official —had moved away from aristocratic forms of theatre. After a brief flirtation with Romantic drama, it settled upon a type of play that reflected the interests and standards of the upper-middle classes who made up the greater part of the audiences. These plays were built according to the formula of the *well-made play*; this gained popularity in the hands of Eugène Scribe (1791–1861), was perfected by his disciple, Victorien Sardou (1831–1908), and dominated not merely a hundred years of French theatre but English drama from Tom Robertson to Terence Rattigan (to the rage of Shaw who, failing to master it himself, dismissed it as 'Sardoodledom' and changed his style). To a conformist writer, the great advantage of this formula, with its rigid control of the way in which character and events develop, its carefully placed confrontation scenes, its perfect unravelling of the plot, was that, with the dénouement, all the problems had to find their solution too. The function of the theatre thenceforth, in so far as it was allowed any serious function at all, was to mirror the prevailing life-style, preoccupations and moral code as closely as the art of theatrical illusion permitted. The audience were thereby confirmed in the inevitability (and eternal survival) of their society.

The classic exponent of this type of play is probably Emile Augier. Augier's plays set out to portray the reality of middle-class life during the Second Empire, defending what he sees as its virtues and criticising its tendency to self-satisfaction and philistinism. In that sense they are intended to be both a description of the status quo and an idealising critique of a particular morality. The main problems of the society are money and class, especially as brought together in the conflict between the aristocracy and the rising bourgeoisie. What Augier tries to promote is a middle course between an aristocratic ethic which, though frivolous and empty, is presented as in some vague way honourable and morally refined, and a bourgeois ethic in which thrift and business honesty are too often sacrificed in practice to greed and the selfish exercise of financial power.

The middle way is not a clear one, for in plays like *Le Gendre de M. Poirier* (1854) and *Le Mariage d'Olympe* (1855) the upper classes are allowed the upper hand. In the first of these, Gaston de Presles, a lazy, trivial but charming nobleman, is set against Poirier, the vulgar draper whose daughter he has married. Gaston is shown as thoughtless and snobbish, Poirier as gross, pushing and absurd, so that it is difficult to side with either of them. Yet when, in the end, Gaston is persuaded to cease sponging off his father-in-law and ill-treating his wife, Antoinette, it is because she permits him to fight a duel in defence of another woman's honour. She has, therefore, adopted Gaston's code, while also persuading him to respect the more restrained virtues of the class into which she was born. *Le Mariage d'Olympe* pits a society prostitute, Olympe Taverney, against the closed family unit of the de Puygirons. Olympe has contrived to make a secret marriage with Henri de Puygiron by concealing her true identity. But her essential vulgarity of character and moral laxity gradually emerge until the old marquis, who is head of the family, is obliged to shoot her to protect its honour. Here too the predominant ethical values are very vaguely delineated, the foremost being the stereotyped virtues of the close-knit family as a domestic unit. Whatever moral position one adopts in relation to the plays, one thing is clear: Augier's idealism is only idealist in a very restricted sense. His morality is a purely materialist one. No metaphysical values are at work in the plays at all. A character is good if he observes the rules of the society in which he lives; since that society is based on capitalist principles, the acquisition and retention of wealth is a perfectly respectable activity if it be done with taste and decorum. What Augier fails to see, and this is what makes the moral centre of his plays so empty, is that the vices he castigates are in large part the natural extension of the virtues he praises. The decision to draw the line between a good thrifty bourgeois who is defending the interests of his family, and a wicked speculator who is exploiting the rest of society for his own benefit, is an arbitrary one, which does no more than confirm the woolly moral assumptions of the audiences for whom Augier was writing.

Though the plays of Alexandre Dumas the younger are more overtly didactic than descriptive, they too depend for their principal values on the portraiture of the moral dilemmas of the contemporary middle class—or, rather, on one particular dilemma, since almost every play promotes the necessity for love and Dumas himself was illegitimate; as a result he was obsessed with sexual misbehaviour and the destructive effects it had, in his view, on both the individual and society. Each play approaches a particular facet of the problem. *Le Fils naturel* (1858) deals with the superior claims of individual merit to accident of birth, and proposes that the law should give the same status to illegitimate and legitimate children. *Les Idées de Madame Aubray* (1867) portrays the dilemma of an idealist whose son falls in love with an unmarried mother; it suggests that a fallen woman who truly puts her past behind her should be rehabilitated by society and allowed to marry a man of honour. *La Femme de Claude* (1873) goes so far as to support the view that an adulteress (admittedly a foreign adventuress and attempted traitor) can justifiably be killed in order to prevent the undermining of the society around her—a fate similar to that of Iza in Dumas' novel *L'Affaire Clemenceau* (1866). In every Dumas play those who transgress against society's rules are presented as morally bad and are usually suitably punished, whether they be dubious financiers (*La Question d'argent*), adulterous women (*Le Demi-Monde*) or adulterous men (*Diane de Lys*), although it is not always clear whether the right person is punished (*Princesse Georges*). Even in *La Dame aux camélias* (1852), the most famous and sympathetic of all his works, which formed the basis for the libretto of Verdi's *La Traviata*, it is significant that Alfred is not allowed to marry the reformed prostitute, Marguerite. We may admire Marguerite's sacrifice of her own happiness for the good of Alfred's family name, but Dumas is careful to kill her off—from tuberculosis—at the very moment when Alfred's father relents and consents to the union. The moral assumption underlying all these plays is, again, that the reconciliation of the happiness of the individual with the smooth functioning of society as it is constitutes the only ultimate goal to be pursued in life. That goal is as exclusively materialist as that of any of Augier's plays.

Zola's objection to Dumas as a playwright was that 'he made himself into the substitute for God on this earth, and as a result the weirdest fancies have come to distort his observational faculties'. By this he means that the overt didactic element warps the representation of social reality. But this didacticism, lacking as it does any metaphysical guarantor, is as representative of a materialist ethic as Zola's own work. A stage farther in the same direction are the plays of Henri Becque, notably *Les Corbeaux* (*c*1872), which Strindberg rather unfairly described as 'simple photography which includes everything'. For materialism in Becque reaches the point at which the author appears to say that the world is as his work describes it, and there is nothing much to be done about it. The attitude is not surprising from a man who could claim that the plays of Molière contained nothing but 'the disinterested knowledge of things human'; and it is an attitude which can be taken to condone the status quo, if one accepts the Marxist critique of all French realists, that they promoted the acceptance of the world by the dispassionate nature of their description. The world which *Les Corbeaux* portrays is that of the financial speculator, the same world that Dumas had analysed in *La Question d'argent* and Augier in *Les Effrontés*. Becque offers us a study of a family, the Vignerons, whose commercial affairs are at a crucial point when the father dies. His two business associates promptly conspire to defraud the wife and daughters; minor creditors get in on the act; prospective suitors to two of the sisters withdraw, and the middle daughter, Marie, is finally obliged to marry Teissier, the principal villain of the piece, to make some reparations to the family fortunes. In its detail *Les Corbeaux* is a more frank and penetrating work than the earlier studies. When first performed (1882) it was considered if anything too realistic, for it made no concessions to the happy ending and the just reward. Indeed, on the first night when, in act III, sc 9, Mme de Saint-Genis informs the youngest Vigneron girl, Blanche, that her son, Georges, is breaking their engagement, although the relationship between the two young lovers has gone farther than propriety could wish, the outraged audience hissed the actress playing Mme de Saint-Genis until she fled from the stage in tears. The truth, it would seem, was not palatable in its entirety. Though the portraiture of corruption and its social consequences was no different from that of the earlier plays, and though the presentation was not, in a strict sense, much more naturalistic, contemporaries were shocked by the openness with which all but material values were rigidly excluded from this mirror of their own world.

The final but not the least significant area of the theatre in which the assumption of a purely material existence forms a basis for the social code portrayed is the great tradition of nineteenth-century farce. Its two most distinguished exponents were Eugène Labiche (1815–88) and Georges Feydeau (1862–1921), though of similar achievement were Meilhac and Halévy whose numerous successes included the libretto for Offenbach's comic operetta *La Belle Hélène* and the play on which Strauss's *Die Fledermaus* was based. The farce of the Second Empire and the early years of the Third Republic comes, paradoxically, as near to questioning the fundamental assumptions of that society as the theatre of the period ever came. For what Augier and Dumas consecrate, and Becque describes, the farce writers at least temporarily subvert. Their targets are social respectability, the family as a unit, the solemnity and self-esteem of the bourgeoisie. Their method—like

Boucicault's in *London Assurance* (1841)—is to upset the patterns which normally order society, and so uncover the frantic efforts of people to maintain convention in a world run riot. Though, in general, in these plays social criticism has passed from an end in itself to a means of providing pure entertainment, they contain a deeper potential meaning, for the characters find themselves in situations where everything follows a nightmare logic which is quite at odds with their own stereotyped realism and reveals the potential irrelevance of their much-vaunted rationality.

A classic example of the genre is Labiche's *Chapeau de paille d'Italie* (1851), where the target is the principle of maintaining social respectability at all cost. A young man, Fadinard, has accidentally allowed his horse to eat the straw hat of Anaïs, a married woman out on a compromising assignation with her lover, Emile. Fadinard feels honour-bound to help Anaïs cover her tracks by replacing her hat, but it is made of Italian straw and apparently unique. Our hero chases off in search of a replacement —to a hat shop, to a soirée and, by chance, to the house of Anaïs's jealous husband. But it is also the day of Fadinard's own marriage and, everywhere he goes, eight carriages containing the entire wedding party trail after him, headed by his intolerable father-in-law. Since none of the party knows the real reason for Fadinard's actions, the plot becomes more and more involved until a final resolution brings the play to the traditional happy close, restoring the status quo. Here the two major elements of Labiche's theatre —marriage and the *ménage-à-trois*—are intertwined, as he pokes fun at the *bon bourgeois* who must keep up the illusion of propriety however irregular the reality of his conduct. Because he is afraid of his prospective father-in-law's moral censure, Fadinard does not explain the truth about the search for the hat. This initial mistake leads to a snowballing of misunderstandings: the milliner to whom he first turns proves to be a former mistress of his; the baroness, to whose house she sends him, takes him to be an Italian tenor; while M Beaupertuis, to whom the baroness refers him, is Anais' husband. Meanwhile the wedding party mistakes the hat-shop for the registry office, the baroness's musical soirée for the wedding reception, M Beaupertuis' house for Fadinard's new apartment and Anais for Fadinard's mistress. The resolution of the chaos owes nothing to the efforts of the characters themselves, but depends entirely on chance. Among the wedding presents is an identical Italian straw hat. The world is thus returned to normality again, as though nothing had happened.

Feydeau at his best takes the technique one step closer to reality. In 1908 he wrote of his own work:

> I noticed that vaudevilles were invariably based on worn-out themes, and false, banal, ridiculous characters: mere puppets. It struck me that each of us, in life, gets mixed up in farcical situations without necessarily losing our individuality in the process ... At once I set about looking for my characters in living reality, determined to preserve their personalities intact. After a comic exposition, I would hurl them into burlesque situations.

This is true of *Puce à l'oreille* (1907). It starts as a mirror of the square, solid, respectable middle-class world, totally sure of itself. The characters are utterly serious, because the comedy derives from the clash between the dignity and morality of the central figures, and the absurdity and impropriety of the events into which they allow themselves to be drawn. Raymonde is almost completely content, secure in her marriage to the director of an insurance company. Her life is sound, predictable and a little dull, while she herself is healthy, adult yet somewhat schoolgirlish in her outlook on relationships. (Feydeau described his heroines as 'breathing virtue till they're out of breath'). Her husband suddenly becomes impotent, but is too embarrassed to explain that this is psychological. She accordingly takes it into her head that he has a mistress. In order to trap him into an assignation, where his infidelity can be unmasked, she persuades her best friend, Lucille, to write him an unsigned note arranging to meet him at an hotel. However, Lucille's husband, a fiery Brazilian, sees the note and recognises his wife's handwriting. Suddenly the safe flirtations and suppressed longings for excitement explode into a mad reality. The small domestic misunderstanding, the white lie which was used to cover it up, together bring about a series of inevitable and appalling disasters. Husbands, wives, mistresses and lovers become so confused that no one is sure whether he or she is being unfaithful or not. Everyone is running so fast that should one of them momentarily arrive in the vaguely hoped-for bed, he is obliged to leap swiftly out again on the other side. Through all this Raymonde and her husband, Chandebise, his best friend, Tournel, and Lucille and her husband retain their rationality like a hat held on desperately in a high wind. Kicked, shot at, unexpectedly embraced, unexpectedly spurned, taken for mad, thwarted by cleft palates or misled by fortuitous resemblances, they continue to behave as though they will inevitably regain control of events in the near future. This belief in common-sense greatly increases the lunacy of the entire situation, until things suddenly unravel themselves, leaving the characters gasping above the highwater-line of bourgeois propriety from which they had been initially and so unexpectedly sucked down.

Feydeau's rigid manipulation of his characters suggests a closed mental system. The world becomes a terrifying place in which human life is horribly attentuated, a rushing from bedroom to bedroom driven on by forces more sinister than any superficial sensuality. But the maniacal aspect is softened, because the verbal and visual humour release our tension in laughter. In a programme note to the National Theatre production of *A Flea in her Ear*, performed in London in 1967–8, Ionesco pointed out how small a step there is between Feydeau's subversion of our acceptance of material reality and what is attempted by the modern Theatre of the Absurd:

Feydeau is a true precursor of the Marx Brothers and other American comedians, in whose work everything starts with apparent casualness, only to end up in a state of demented precipitation—which may well be an accurate caricature of our own agitation, our gallop towards the abyss.

But with the Marx Brothers and Laurel and Hardy everything is destroyed, smashed to pieces; their madness is more poetic and menacing. With Feydeau, the madness is sweetened; he doesn't wish to frighten us. But nowadays, we have learned to look more deeply and to be unnerved by what we see.

In that sense, we may regard Labiche and Feydeau as taking an exclusively material world and experimenting with the suggestion that pragmatism is an inadequate account of the experience of life, only to return at the end to confirming the audience's assumption that the world will ultimately always conform to the accepted way of looking at things. The materialist approach, far from being undermined, is in effect reinforced.

It is not intended to suggest in any way that the writers whose plays we have been discussing were interested in positivism or any other philosophical system. But the emphasis on the reality—usually the exclusive reality—of material phenomena which underlies everything from Comte's social theories to Bernard's description of scientific method is only a more serious example of the same concern with life on a purely material plane which under-lies the plays of Augier, Dumas, Becque and the farce writers. It is, however, in the novel that a conscious use of scientific principles is to be found at this period, notably in the works of Balzac, Zola and Maupassant. Here we can reasonably speak of influences, for Balzac's attitude to the study of man as a social animal was directly influenced by the work of the biologist Geoffroy Saint-Hilaire, and Zola's theories were based on Claude Bernard's *Introduction to the Study of Experimental Medicine*.

SCIENCE AND THE THEORY OF THE NOVEL

Balzac

Balzac has set out his views quite clearly in the Foreword (1842) to *La Comédie humaine*. The function of the novelist is parallel to that of the zoologist, who analyses the nature and organisation of the animal kingdom. This kingdom Balzac presents according to Saint-Hilaire's view of the origin of species:

> There is only one animal. The Creator used only one single model for all organised beings. An animal is a principle that takes its outer form from the environment in which it finds itself obliged to develop. It is from differences of environment that the various zoological species result.

Species in human society is similarly controlled by milieu, and is defined by such considerations as occupation:

> Does not society make out of man, according to the differences of environment in which different people move, as many types of man as there are species in zoology? The differences between a soldier, a workman, an administrator, a lawyer, a gentleman of leisure, an intellectual, a politician, a tradesman, a sailor, a poet, a pauper, a priest are, though more difficult to put one's finger on, as considerable as those which mark the distinction between the wolf, the lion, the donkey, the crow, the shark, the seal, the sheep etc. There have, then, always been, and there always will be, social species, just as there are zoological species. If Buffon has done a first class job in his attempt to get down on paper the whole of zoology, is there not a task of the same order to be carried out for society?

The task of the zoologist of the human kingdom is in fact harder than Buffon's, for there are many complications in the defining of the human species. A woman, for example, is not necessarily merely the female equivalent of a man, but may belong to a species of her own. And the concept of evolution, which is only as yet a hypothesis in the biological sciences, is a more serious proposition in the social world, where social barriers can be transcended and habits modified from epoch to epoch.

This general biological approach to the study of society reflects itself in the grouping which Balzac gave to the vast corpus of his work. Its threefold major division into studies of manners, philosophical studies and analytical studies is broken down again, in the case of the major section on manners, into scenes from private life, from provincial life, from Parisian life, from political life, from military life, and country life. Then, within these sections, there are suggestive subdivisions, such as single people (provincial life) and poor relations (Parisian life). In a letter to his mistress, Mme Hanska, in 1834, Balzac defined the relations of the three major divisions: the studies of manners were to represent the effects, the primary data of a scientific observation of society; the philosophical studies were to be the causes deduced from these effects; and the analytical studies were to show the principles derived from these causes. What Balzac meant by 'principles' in this context is obscure, but the care with which he sought to order his scientific study is evident.

Balzac's scientific approach is not confined to his overall vision of the work as a sociological study. His concept of character and its assessment owed much to the theories of Lavater on physiognomy and of Gall on phrenology—theories which have long been exposed as absurd, but which Balzac (like the young George Eliot) accepted as scientific truths. All these elements of scientific doctrine on the physiology of the individual, the relationship of individual to milieu, and the structuring of small units into the social whole follow a straightforward positivist pattern, in which the whole pattern of events is governed by a complicated process of cause and effect—that is, a scientific determinism such as is proposed by Claude Bernard. The best-known part of this, in Balzac's novels, is probably the determinant relationship between environment and character of which the author himself in his *Traité de la vie élégante* said: 'The world around one is a sort of organised system which represents a man as closely as the colours of a snail are reproduced on its shell.' To this view (which can be closely paralleled in the novels of Thomas Hardy) we owe that curiously cinematic technique by which so many of Balzac's novels begin, panning in through the description of a place until, by the time we focus on the individuals within it, we already know what their temperament will be. Not just places, but clothes, facial expressions and habits of life are all revealing of the inner man. So *Le Cousin Pons* starts with a long description of eccentric items of clothing which represent poor Pons within them. In *Père Goriot* the famous portrait of the Pension Vauquer prepares us similarly for the seedy and run-down collection of its inmates. This determinism is carried through to the explanation of all substantial psychological detail. When Mme Birotteau undergoes her prophetic nightmare at the opening of *César Birotteau*, in which she sees her own double in abject poverty beseeching her for alms, Balzac comments:

> Fear is a half-morbific feeling, which exerts such violent pressure on the human machine that its faculties are suddenly either lifted to the highest degree of their power, or reduced to their lowest degree of disorganisation. Physiology has long been surprised by this phenomenon which overturns its systems and knocks down its theories, although it is only the internal equivalent of a lightning flash, but, like all electrical accidents, bizarre and whimsical in its ways. This explanation will become commonplace as soon as intellectuals recognise the immense role played by electricity in human thought.

The determinism which is here used to explain the functioning of the individual is the structural force which allows Balzac to present social groups as products of race, environment and way of life, in a way which made him seem, to the later nineteenth century, the prime realist. This is, of course, a very one-sided view of the novels, for the realism was strongly tempered by a visionary streak, but it does represent what was for Balzac himself a very important part of his role as author.

Zola

Zola's approach to scientific method in literature is very much modelled on Balzac's, though his acknowledged master as theorist was Claude Bernard. Yet the relationship posited between the professions of novelist and of clinical researcher is a quite unacceptable one, for the novelist has a power over the development of his characters that the doctor—mercifully—lacks over his patients. As it is almost certain that Zola had not read Bernard's *Introduction to the Study of Experimental Medicine* when he began to write the Rougon-Macquart cycle of novels, his scientific approach can more profitably be related to the teachings of Hippolyte Taine, whose determinist approach to psychology is central to most of his writings, and to such pseudo-scientific works as Prosper Lucas' *Treatise on Natural Heredity* (1847–50). Zola took as the significant factors in the development of the individual, and thence of society as a whole, Taine's 'race, milieu, moment', and proposed that the novelist should make himself the creative analyst of social reality by using these features as the initial determining factors for the social and psychological exploration that was to constitute each novel. So, in *The Experimental Novel* (1880) Zola maintains that the function of the Naturalist novelist is to accept the facts as determined, to deduce as much as he can from them, and only to exercise intuition and go ahead of science when he reached beyond the available facts into the unknown. Since heredity and environment and their effects on the individual were as yet hardly opened up by science, the novelist had to take the risk of exceeding reality, but if he incorporated as much observed fact as he could into the literary structure he would remain adequately scientific.

In the case of the Rougon-Macquart cycle, with its twenty novels chronicling the fortunes of a single family, and its ramifications under the Second Empire—and, in practice, the early Third Republic—Zola seeks to establish certain traits, including alcoholism and nervous disorders, as endemic in the family line, and show what effect the contact with a variety of milieu has on each member of the family. In fact, in the majority of the novels it is the milieu which dominates—the portrayal of the different worlds constituting the disparate structure of France under Louis-Napoléon. In *Germinal*, Etienne's family history is of much less interest than the circumstances of the mining community; just as, in *La Terre*, Jean's background is insignificant in relation to the power of the land over the peasant communities who live by it. This is not to say that heredity is not frequently called into play, even for minor characters, but—as in Dickens's *Bleak House*—it becomes subordinated to the social interest of the environment as a determinant feature on individual development.

It has already been noted that the materialist side of Balzac, though essential to his art, is only a single facet of his thought. In Zola's case the same is true. It is even dubious whether Zola—unlike Balzac—believed in the scientific value of the theories which he used. A propos of his compositional methods, he noted (strictly for private consumption):

> Must always use logical deduction. Doesn't matter whether generating fact is recognised as totally true . . . But when the fact has been posited, and I have accepted it as axiomatic, must then mathematically deduce the whole volume from it, and then be absolutely truthful.

In another similar note he shows that his aim in selecting his scientific base was above all to provide a working artistic framework:

> Assume a dominant philosophical tendency not for didactic purposes, but to give my books unity. Best possibly would be materialism, by which I mean the belief in forces which would never need explaining. Nothing compromising about the word *force*. No longer possible to use the word destiny which would be ridiculous over ten volumes.

Equally well the faith in human progress which emerges, apparently contradictorily, from the gloom of many of the novels implies an idealistic streak at odds with the professed role of scientific observer. But not, perhaps, at odds with the general development of the scientific movement in nineteenth-century France. For the positivists were, with the exception of Bernard, by no means so scientific, so detached from the idealist movements in society, as they proclaimed. In linking the name of science with visionary elements, Balzac and Zola were by no means out of tune with the way in which supposedly materialist thought had been developing from the writings of Comte onward.

The philosophers

To say that Comte was not a proper positivist is rather like claiming that a 'Granny Smith' is not a real apple. If not, what is? But, if measured by the standards of Claude Bernard or the English positivists like J. S. Mill, Comte's thought is riddled with idealist leaps. The background against which he developed his theory is certainly in part responsible. He wants to contribute to the building of a stable social order, and to that end he creates a formula for new intellectual bases to society. Science is therefore a means to an end, and runs the risk of being subordinated to that end. Some of the peculiarities of his thought can be traced to an acceptance of 'scientific' ideas, such as phrenology, that now seem merely eccentric; more serious are the substantial distortions of method, even in *The Course of Positivist Philosophy* itself. One of Comte's principles is that empirical observation is useful only as the testing ground for hypotheses which will in turn yield proven laws of human conduct. This is a legitimate principle in itself, but soon degenerates into an acceptance of *a priori* assumptions that the collecting of observed phenomena is meant to illustrate, a procedure which, by the end of *The Course*, he seems to think is legitimate and necessary for a sociologist. In Comte's own practice this means selecting only those facts that happen to fit a pet theory, a charge which can be held against even some of his fundamental tenets. For example, when Comte proposes that the course of human history is directed by ideas, the only proof he offers is the dogmatic statement:

> I shall never believe that it is necessary for me to prove to the readers of this work that ideas direct and overthrow the world, or, to put it another way, that the whole mechanism of society rests in the last analysis on opinions. My readers will above all be aware that the great moral and political crisis of present-day societies results, in the last analysis, from intellectual anarchy.

Yet if the so-called 'law of the three estates' is to apply to sociology, Comte needs to prove that intellectual history has the relationship to social history which he asserts. If his assumption cannot be proven, his entire promotion of positivist philosophy becomes irrelevant to the social ends which he is pursuing.

Comte's real problem is that he is seeking rules for the development of society and not in-depth analysis of society as it is. As D. G. Charlton has put it: 'In the last resort he prefers false laws to no laws at all.' Nowhere is this more plain than when Comte moves from laying down the ways in which sociology must develop, in order to predict the direction of social change in the future, to proposing a particular ethical code. Already in the later books of *The Course* he is asserting that the natural development of society is toward altruism. Just as, according to Lamarck's theory of acquired characteristics, animals have gained physical attributes which are useful to them, so man has gradually been acquiring moral qualities and intellectual powers favourable to the establishment of general happiness. This leap of unreason is based on the assumption that what, according to sociological thinking, is most likely to happen is also morally desirable. Accordingly, Comte is inventing a metaphysical entity and setting it up as a scientific objective, so that in his later *System of Positivist Politics* a new science, morality, is created, on the principle that man should live for the good of his fellow man. The details of Comte's social prescriptions, seeking to impose an authoritarian political and (in a humanistic sense) religious creed for the common good, are not significant in themselves. But the way in which the enthusiastic proponent of scientific method becomes a metaphysical idealist—no more rational than Victor Hugo in the vision of the universe he propounded in *Légende des siècles*—is symptomatic of what happened to all the major materialist thinkers of the century.

What in Comte is a growing tendency towards the illusions of idealism is in Ernest Renan a permanent feature. A jaundiced contemporary observed: 'He gives his generation what they want —infinity-flavoured sweets', and the critique, though unkind, pinpoints the incoherence of Renan as a thinker. All his adult life, until the disillusion and frivolous scepticism of his final years, he was torn by the desire to reconcile religion and science. The compromise between new scientific discoveries and the more elastic doctrines of Protestantism that permitted English thinkers to remain within Christianity was not open to Renan. Tennyson in 'De profundis' accepts a simple parallelism in the 'two greetings' which compose the poem. For Renan such an assimilation was impossible. He tried to maintain two separate faiths, one of the soul, one of the reason; but the Christian faith as such could have no part in his philosophy, because its essential supernatural element could never have been scientifically verified, and he saw, accordingly, no reason to postulate that it ever existed. What he attempts to substitute for the Catholicism of his youth is scientism, a religion of science in which the traditional concepts of religion can be reconciled with the critical spirit of scientific method. This is the import of all his work from *The Future of Science* right through to the *Philosophical Dialogues*. His basic proposition is that scientific method can be used to expand knowledge until we have complete knowledge of the universe, not only in its physical but also in its metaphysical and ethical aspects. God is, then, perfect knowledge, and the attainment of perfect knowledge is therefore equivalent to the creation of God and the identifying of the self with him. Unlike Comte, the science that Renan sees as the key to knowledge is not sociology but *philologie* in the rather southern European sense of 'the science of the products of the human mind'.

By studying the past in cultural terms the *philologue* will be able to establish the steps by which the human mind has evolved, and predict the direction that it needs to take. Renan's own analysis of the history of man's mind in *Letter to Berthelot* is designed to show that human development is historically in the direction of greater consciousness, which will lead to the attainment of the desired perfect knowledge.

In all this the assumptions, leaps and intuitions are endless. Even in his concept of scientific method, Renan moves away from the conventionally scientific to admit imagination and intuition as valid means for the acquisition of knowledge. Admittedly this makes him in some ways a more advanced thinker than his contemporaries, for it shows an awareness of the complexity of human response to the phenomena of the material world which is quite lacking in the pure materialists. Yet such an attitude is also a loophole by which the poetry of metaphysics, as he himself described it, can be brought by stealth into the process of factual analysis. However, the major leap in Renan's thought, as in Comte's, is not this assimilation of different kinds of 'knowledge' to the same status as empirical evidence; it is the move from description of things as they are to prescription of things as they should be. Renan assumes that the direction in which humanity has moved so far must be a desirable one, and that therefore to continue to move in that direction is progress towards absolute good. When, in the *Philosophical Dialogues and Fragments*, he tries to defend why the evolution is necessarily a good one, and why man must necessarily undergo it, he is reduced to two quite contradictory arguments: the first—on the assumption that 'evil is to revolt against nature . . . her purpose is good; let us will what she wills'—is that man has free choice but a moral duty to further nature's ends; the second is that, as nature works according to general laws that are never suspended, man has no choice but is compelled to further nature's ends, whether he likes it or not. This is a simple example of the way in which, as a structure of rationally conceived arguments, Renan's philosophy is a non-starter. As a profession of faith in man and his future, in the nature and function of the universe, and in the powers of the human mind, it is a fascinating demonstration of how easily lyrical idealism could usurp the entrenched materialist standpoint of the positivist-trained thinkers.

A similar fusion of idealism and science also marks the man who, in purely literary terms at least, was probably the most influential of the positivists. Hippolyte Taine's range of academic work was prodigious. *The History of English Literature* (1864), *The Origins of Contemporary France* (1875–93) and *The Philosophy of Art* (1882) are the three most notable examples. The work that symbolises in itself the unity of method and purpose underlying all his writings is *On Intelligence*, in which he examines human psychology and its functioning. For what he examines in the study of social history, literary history or art history are the workings of the human mind as manifested in the objects it creates or the events it controls. By this he hopes to reveal how complete knowledge may eventually be achieved, an aim not unlike Renan's. He is reputed to have said to his nephew: 'I think that with sufficient data, such as perfected instruments and thorough observation will be able to provide, it will be possible to have total knowledge of man and life. There is no definitive mystery.' The total of knowledge attained through the individual sciences will contribute to the new 'complete' science, metaphysics, which will explain the necessary relationships of all material phenomena to the absolute. In order to achieve this, man has to take the positivist method and make it applicable to metaphysics—in other words, to synthesise the two great opposing forces of nineteenth-century thought: physical surfaces and the worlds of the mind, reality and dream.

Taine's method is genuinely scientific in origin. He insists throughout his work on the principle that sense-data must provide the basis for all our knowledge of reality. From the study of groups of facts one must establish the causes or laws determining the relationship of phenomena, the most famous example of such a law in Taine's own work being the factors of *race*, *milieu*, *moment* which he proposes as the determiners of literary composition in his *Introduction to the History of English Literature*. It is curious that a method so objective as Taine's should give rise to works whose particular brand of universalism seems to the modern eye hardly less personal than the lyrical subjectivity with which a Michelet wrote his *Histoire de France*. The cause is a fundamental flaw in Taine's scientific method; he ceases to regard his laws as working hypotheses, and begins to treat them as absolute knowledge, as facts in themselves. This opens the way to his construction of a 'scientific' metaphysics. He proposes the construction of a hierarchy of knowledge, by grouping causes until we can abstract from them the cause of causes, and so on back to the supreme cause: 'This is the point at which one feels the concept of nature being born within one . . . At the very summit of things, at the utmost height of the inaccessible luminous ether, the eternal axiom expresses itself, and the prolonged echo of this creative formula composes the immensity of the universe with its inexhaustible undulations' (*The Philosophers of Nineteenth-century France*). This pantheistic view of nature is as lyrical and non-rational in conception as the God-substitute to which Renan's science will supposedly lead us, although Taine does not erect either a religious or an ethical system around his metaphysical supreme cause. When critics attacked his system, he replied that he had none. Nevertheless he was willing to express a quite ungrounded faith in the future achievements of scientific method and its ability to reveal ultimate truths: 'In this use of science and in this conception of things there is a new art, a new ethics, a new political science, a new religion and it is our task today to discover them.' His scientism is more guarded in its formulation than Renan's, but equally thorough-going.

The creative artists

The striking feature about the adherents of science, reason and the study of material phenomena in France of the mid-century is their eagerness to move from the practical to the idealist. Indeed, the proper division between Chateaubriand and Hugo on the one hand and the positivists on the other is that the latter built their ideals on an attachment to the material world as we experience it conventionally, whereas the former created their ideals from the dream of how they would like the world to be. So that when the philosophical reaction to positivism comes, with Henri Bergson, it will attack the reliability of material phenomena as an account of reality, rather than the use the positivists made of that reality. Now, if Comte, Renan and Taine are, in their different ways, as much subject to illusion as the great Romantics, how much more natural that creative artists, such as Leconte de Lisle, Balzac or Zola, who also make great play with the observational basis of what they write, should similarly conceal vision, illusion and ideal within the surfaces of the material world they portray. Leconte de Lisle may look out of place in this list, and indeed he is in so far as he has no enthusiasm for the present or future of mankind, and none of the sense of inevitable human progress that marks Renan and Zola. Moreover, his theoretical statements on poetry consistently stress the function of poetry as a quite un-positivist vision of absolute truth, a unique means to attain knowledge of the ideal. But many of his poems themselves have an appearance of total concern with material surfaces which has led him to be viewed as a materialist poet. One of the most famous attacks on his poetry for precisely this quality was delivered by, of all people, Alexandre Dumas the younger, under the guise of an official speech of congratulation to Leconte de Lisle on his election to the Académie française in 1886:

> You have immolated all personal emotion within yourself, you
> have conquered all passion, obliterated all sensation, stifled all

feeling ... Impassive, glittering and unchangeable, like an antique mirror of polished silver, you have seen the passage of worlds, deeds, ages, external objects, and you have recorded them just as they were ... You do not want poets to talk to us of the things of the soul ... No more emotion, no more ideals, no more faith, no more beating hearts, no more tears. You make the sky a desert and the earth silent.

In accusing Leconte de Lisle of subordinating emotion to intellect and of confining poetry to the reflection of the external world either in its synchronic form of biological and mineral entities or in its diachronic form of historical facts, Dumas is essentially accusing him of excluding ideals, and indeed ideas, in favour of mere phenomena.

It is, of course, easy to make this charge look silly by quoting a poem like 'To Modern Man' (*Poèmes barbares*), in which the poet violently and directly attacks his own generation for its lack of imagination and crass materialism:

> *Hommes, tueurs de Dieux, les temps ne sont pas loin*
> *Où, sur un grand tas d'or vautrés dans quelque coin,*
> *Ayant rongé le sol nourricier jusqu'aux roches*
>
> *Ne sachant faire rien ni des jours ni des nuits,*
> *Noyés dans le néant des suprêmes ennuis,*
> *Vous mourrez bêtement en emplissant vos poches.*

[Men, killers of Gods, the time is not far off when, wallowing in some corner on a great heap of gold, having gnawed the breast of the life-giving earth down to the very rocks, Not knowing what to do with the days or the nights, drowned in the nullity of ultimate boredom, you will die stupidly as you fill your pockets.]

It is equally possible to show the inadequacy of Dumas's view in relation to poems which superficially fulfil his description. Take, for example, 'Polar Landscape', a poem added to the second edition of *Poèmes barbares* in 1878:

> *Un monde mort, immense écume de la mer,*
> *Gouffre d'ombre stérile et de lueurs spectrales,*

Jets de pics convulsifs étirés en spirales
Qui vont éperdument dans le brouillard amer.

Un ciel rugueux roulant par blocs, un âpre enfer
Où passent à plein vol les clameurs sépulcrales,
Les rires, les sanglots, les cris aigus, les râles
Qu'un vent sinistre arrache à son clairon de fer.

Sur les hauts caps branlants, rongés des flots voraces,
Se roidissent les Dieux brumeux des vieilles races,
Congelés dans leur rêve et leur lividité;

Et les grands ours, blanchis par les neiges antiques,
Çà et là, balançant leurs cous épileptiques,
Ivres et monstrueux, bavent de volupté.

[A dead world, immense foam of the sea, abyss of sterile shadow and spectral lights, convulsive fountains of peaks drawn up in spirals going distractedly off into the bitter mist. A corrugated sky rolling in blocks, a raw hell where sepulchral cries pass in full flight, the laughter, sobs, piercing calls, death-rattles which a sinister wind tears from its iron bugle. On the heights of the tottering headlands, gnawed away by the voracious waves, the misty gods of the old races stiffen, frozen in their dream and their lividity; And the great bears, whitened by the snows of antiquity, here and there, swinging their epileptic necks to and fro, drunken and monstrous, drool with lustful pleasure.]

Ostensibly this sonnet is a purely descriptive poem, impersonally evoking a polar landscape. As soon as one begins to concentrate on the imagery, not only does one detect an interpretative re-arrangement of the elements of the scenery to create emotional effects, but one realises too that the images rapidly develop beyond physical reality. The 'abyss of sterile shadow' in the first stanza contains approximately one and a half physical facts: the half-light of the landscape and the scooping of the ice into undulations; beyond that, it has all the extra associations of *gouffre*, a bottomless pit, the pit of hell, a whirlpool, and the overriding word of the phrase is *stérile*, the absence of life or the ability to create life. In the two opening lines of the sonnet, the dominant impression is not visual at all, but abstract—death, barrenness, infinity. From then on the imagery becomes wilder, more 'surreal'. Obviously there is a physically discernible basis to the idea of a corrugated sky relentlessly surging forward in great segments, or to the image of the screaming of the wind as a death rattle played on a bugle. But the major effect is of violence and pain, of the absence of man and the animacy of the inhuman physical world. The climax of the sonnet is the image of the 'misty gods of the old races' stiffening and congealing on the caps of icefloes. Here the pictorial element dissolves entirely into Blakean nightmare. The polar landscape is a symbol of the end of the world, the end of the universe, an idea that Leconte de Lisle probably picked up from Lamarck or the post-Darwinian biologists, who saw the natural end of evolution as cosmic death. The congealing gods are the whole range of human mythology, and the natural forces which it symbolises, finally brought to extinction. The poem closes on a grotesque image—that of the only remaining living creatures, monstrous polar bears—a parody of life, an ultimate degeneration of organic matter. So that, although a first glance might suggest that this poem is merely a mirror of a given material phenomenon, it is in fact the vehicle for the apocalyptic vision of a pessimist philosophy.

Whether we look at the nature poems for which Leconte de Lisle is best known, or at the short narrative poems on historical and oriental subjects, the same use of facts to disguise a deeply felt metaphysical belief runs through most of his work. In poems like 'The Jaguar' or 'The Sleep of the Condor' the fascination with the theme of nature without man, with the point at which life slips over into death, exceeds what is essential to the animal portraiture and becomes a symbol of the poet's own obsession with impassivity as a rehearsal for the nothingness that follows death. In the same way, the stories reconstructed from Greek, Scandinavian or Eastern mythology, though superficially scientific in their blending of scholarly sources, archaising of name forms and objective narrative manner, all reflect a particular philosophical position: the revolt against a destiny that seems to bind mankind to expiation for crimes it was fated to commit, and that preparation for Nirvana which is the dignified response of the sage to the nullity of existence. It would be misleading perhaps to talk about idealism in the context of such poetry, for Leconte de Lisle subscribed to Vigny's view of life as '*Un triste accident entre deux sommeils infinis*'—the epigrammatic turn of phrase is difficult to catch in English, but the idea is of a 'sad accident interjected into an eternal sleep'. There is an undeniable blend of metaphysical anguish with recording of material surfaces—a blend not without its similarities to the tensions in the positivist philosophers who were the poet's contemporaries. For a similar amalgam of science and religion in English poetry one would look to Tennyson, but the poetic manner of the two poets is very different.

The same blend can be traced in a very different form in the novels of Balzac. We have already looked briefly at the scientific method behind *La Comédie humaine* and at the significance of scientific determinism for Balzac's presentation of character and milieu. The forces which animate Balzac's world, and the philosophy that underlies them, are anything but scientific in modern terms; though Balzac sincerely believed in their scientific value, notions like phrenology and mesmerism have long since been disproved. What Balzac's philosophy discloses is a scientism *avant la lettre*, where intuitional and occult elements have been admitted to the status of facts in the same way that Renan and Taine were to allow metaphysical concepts into their theories. Balzac's excuse is the purely aesthetic one that his ideas serve to animate a fictional world; but there is no suggestion, as there is with Zola, that he did not hold by the complete truth of every pseudo-scientific or illuminist theory he brings into play in the novels.

The novels that hold the key for our understanding of what Balzac believed are *Peau de chagrin* (1831) and *Louis Lambert*

(1835); these predate the writing of all his major works. *Peau de chagrin* is that curiosity, a supernatural tale about contemporary society. Raphael, a young man about to commit suicide, strays into an antique shop whose mysterious elderly owner gives him a piece of wild ass's skin on which King Solomon had cast a spell. Whoever owns it will be granted every wish he makes; but with each wish both the skin and its possessor's life-span will shrink. To test the power of the skin the incredulous Raphael calls for an orgy, and immediately falls in with a group of young men who lead him off to a wild dinner party. The aftermath of this event, which gives Balzac an opportunity for satire at the expense of venal journalism and political corruption as well as the more obvious social targets, also provides an occasion for a flashback into the events leading up to Raphael's proposed suicide. The account maps out the difficulty of attaining social success for a man without substantial means, and the corrosion of hope and of the ability to love which occurs in the pursuit of such success. At the end of his story Raphael puts the ass's skin to the test once more. He comes round after the orgy to the news that an unexpected inheritance has made him immensely rich. At the same time he notices that the skin has already shrunk. The third part of the novel then recounts his desperate attempts to avoid willing anything, in order to preserve the skin and, with it, his life. His efforts are in vain, and eventually he dies in an erotic frenzy, his last act of will, in the arms of the woman he loves.

The ass's skin here is the symbol of the vital energy which Balzac considers each individual possesses; it is according to his or her temperament whether and how that energy is expended or conserved. To over-extend oneself, as César Birotteau does in the eponymous novel, when he turns from honest commerce to the hazards of speculation, is to court disaster. As the usurer Gigonnet says of him, ambiguously: '*Il n'est pas de force*' (he's not up to strength). In *Peau de chagrin* the nature of this energy is analysed by the antique dealer:

I shall reveal a great mystery of human life to you in a few words. Man exhausts himself by two acts that are instinctively accomplished which dry up the springs of his existence. Two words express all the forms taken by these two sources of death, *will* and *power*. Between these two bounds of human action there is another formula which sages have appropriated, and to it I owe the good fortune of my longevity. *Will* burns us up and *power* destroys us, but *knowledge* leaves our weak organism in a perpetual state of peace.

The old man has preserved his vital energy by retiring into his brain and by restricting thought to observation. Raphael, by contrast, expends his energies wildly. The way he tears himself apart is symptomatic of the way all the members of his society, and, by implication, of society in general, tear themselves apart in the pursuit of power and of the money which symbolises that power.

The concept of vital energy, of will and power, is a moral one, whose use in *Peau de chagrin* could be accounted purely symbolic. In *Louis Lambert* Balzac expands explicitly on the metaphysical aspects of these and related concepts. Louis is presented as a school-fellow of the author; he possesses peculiar powers of inner contemplation and of philosophical speculation. He and the young Balzac, isolated from their school mates by a gulf of incomprehension, are taken up with trying to discover the nature of thought and how it is generated. Balzac is portrayed as supporting a materialist view and Louis a mystical one, in which spirit and matter are independent entities; but the two views together represent the way Balzac the author is trying to reconcile opposites and produce a unified concept of the nature of thought. The novel relates Louis' draft of a *Treatise on Will* which proposes the possibility that the mind possesses the potential power to overstep the normal limits prescribed by the laws of time and space. This *Treatise* adopts a *soi-disant* physiological explanation of the two phenomena of will and thought. The scientific basis for this is the theory of Mesmer, according to which thought expresses itself in ideas that are a fluid, similar to electric current or light waves. Will similarly expresses itself in acts of willing that have a physical reality as yet not measurable by science. The more control an individual has over thought, the more he can spiritualise himself. The more control he has over will, the greater his power to influence the world outside himself. Louis Lambert takes the former course; he becomes more and more enclosed in a world of inner contemplation, approaching a mystical comprehension of ultimate truths. Despite a brief reaction and attempt to revert to purely scientific studies, he is finally drawn to the study of the Swedish mystic, Swedenborg. The stress which this development of the inner man places on his outward physical existence becomes too great and, when he falls in love, the sensual implications of his passion are so totally at odds with his 'soaring through the world of the spirit' that he finally breaks down, goes into a three-year cataleptic trance and dies.

The theosophist aspects of this philosophy Balzac was to carry to more absurd lengths in *Séraphita*. But the central concepts of will and thought were to provide him with the basis for all his major characters. Already, in *Peau de chagrin*, Raphael de Valentin has explained to the Countess Fedora the power that the concentration of will gives a man over his fellow creatures:

> She seemed greatly diverted to learn that the human will was a material force in the same way as steam is; that in the moral world nothing could resist this force when a man was accustomed to concentrate it, to manipulate its totality, to direct this fluid mass constantly on to the souls of others; that such a man could modify anything at will relative to mankind, even the absolute laws of nature.

Here is the key to the Balzacian superman. Talent alone is not enough, if a man cannot concentrate and impose his will in this way. But the man who has this total self-control will manipulate society as he wishes, as does Vautrin, the ex-convict. When he first appears, in *Père Goriot*, Vautrin explains his philosophy of domination to his intended pupil, Eugène de Rastignac, who, though he rejects this advice at the time, has already learnt by the end of the novel how to manipulate other people in his own interests, and will go on, in the *La Maison Nucingen*, to show himself an adept pupil of the doctrine of self-interest. In *Illusions perdues* Vautrin repeats the same advice to Lucien de Rubempré, and proceeds to manipulate him in his own battle with society. Eventually, in *Splendeurs et misères des courtisanes*, he reveals his domination over the counter-society of the criminal world. This domination Vautrin achieves through the double power of omniscience and omnipotence which stems from the right use of will.

In others, all the passions become concentrated into a single obsession—very often an obsession with money, for money is the symbol of power in the venal modern world. Hence the power relished by moneylenders like Gobseck and bankers like the Baron de Nucingen. Gobseck's method of enjoying life, as he tells Derville in *Gobseck*, is voyeurist:

> All human passions, magnified by the way your social interests affect them, come and parade before me as I live in a state of calm ... In a word, I hold the world in my hand without the least cost to my energies, and the world does not have the slightest hold on me.

His energy is never really expended in the exercise of power, just as, symbolically, his money is never really expended, for it returns to him with interest. For a study in miniature of the social power of money and of the man who possesses it, we can turn to *Eugénie Grandet* (on which Henry James modelled *Washington Square*). Grandet, the miser, manipulates his immediate family as effectively as the Parisian moneylenders and bankers pull the strings of all society:

> As in all misers, there was to be found in him a persistent need to match himself against other men and win their money legally. Is not to impose on others a way of giving proof of one's power, of perpetually giving oneself the right to despise those who, in their

excessive weakness, allow themselves to be devoured, here on earth?

Usurers and misers are a special category of monomaniacs in that they are hoarders of strength. In many other cases, as with old Goriot's obsession with paternal love or César Birotteau's with probity, the result of monomania is the expenditure of all one's supply of vital energy, and consequent self-destruction. Even where this concentration of thought and will is not consistently channelled into a single aim, the effect of a violent single emotion can be fatal to the person experiencing it, as with Mme de Mortsauf in *Le Lys dans la vallée* whose spasm of jealousy at her platonic lover's infidelity brings on an apparent stomach cancer which swiftly kills her. However, the husbanding of energies is not an answer in itself. Félix de Vandenesse, in the same novel, by his voluntary chastity (or sexual indifference) dries himself up emotionally and destroys the women with whom he comes into contact.

What holds good for the individual must also hold good for society. As Balzac wrote in *Cousin Pons*: 'Everything hangs together in the real world. Every movement in it corresponds to a cause, every cause is connected to the whole, and consequently, the whole is represented by the slightest movement.' The way the laws of the human mind, as Balzac sees them, function, can be responsible for good or ill in society as a whole. His good characters, such as Eve Séchard in *Illusions perdues* or César Birotteau, usually destroy themselves in their attempt to combat the destructive effects of society, or at least save only a very little from the general ruin. Within society as at present constituted, the laws of the human mind lead usually to the pursuit of the individual's good—ie egotism—at the expense of the general good. As he expresses it at the end of *Le Curé de Tours*:

We live in a period when the fault of governments is to have not so much fashioned society for man as to have tailored man to society.

There exists a permanent struggle between the individual and the society which wants to exploit him, and which he in his turn attempts to exploit for his own profit; whereas in the old days men, who were in fact freer, showed a more disinterested attitude toward the common weal.

In so far as Balzac adopts a moral stance in the novels, it is to condemn this evil mutual influence of society and individual. Everything which undermines corporate institutions, such as the family, is to be condemned. Young men, like Lucien de Rubempré in *Illusions perdues*, who ruin their families in the pursuit of personal fame and fortune, or old men, like Goriot, who indulge their children to the point at which the exercise of paternal affection becomes paradoxically destructive are equally reprehensible. The supreme example of the egoist in this context is, of course, the bachelor or spinster who, in Balzac's eyes, has conserved his or her energy only to expend it on self-indulgence. Balzac's classic study of this is found in *Le Curé de Tours*. This long short-story stages the conflict of three egoists: the Abbé Birotteau, his spinster landlady Sophie Gamard, and his secret opponent, the Abbé Troubert. By setting in the small community closely linked with the cathedral of Saint-Gatien this story of the way the three individuals affect one another's lives, the author exposes how the rigid social groupings of provincial society respond to the smallest events. By making two of the main characters priests he also reveals the spiritual bankruptcy of the contemporary church— as, on a more tempered level, does Charlotte Brontë in *Shirley*. Birotteau has no spiritual dimension at all. His secret monomania is the entirely material desire to possess a certain set of lodgings within the cathedral precincts. This objective achieved, he concentrates on the attainment of a canonry. His downfall comes because he has no capacity to look beyond himself, and accordingly fails to take into account the social ambitions of Mlle Gamard. Birotteau is an amiable fool; Sophie Gamard is a warped personality:

Spinsters, never having tailored their characters and their lives to the pattern of another life or to the characters of others, as destiny requires that a woman should, have, for the most part, a mania for wanting to subordinate everything around them to themselves. In Mlle Gamard this feeling degenerated into despotism.

Her obsessive desire is to set up a little *salon* of her own, to rival the other ladies of the town. Birotteau unwittingly builds up her hopes that he can contribute to this by bringing in aristocratic contacts, and equally unwittingly destroys her hopes by abandoning her 'evenings' when he gets bored with her. From then on she devotes herself simply and solely to his destruction. More interesting than either of these is the third egoist, Abbé Troubert; he has all Birotteau's materialist aims, and more. He covets Birotteau's lodgings, he covets the same canonry to which Birotteau aspires. Unlike his simple, easygoing fellow-cleric, Troubert is ruthless, for he has learnt the secret of imposing his will. Through him Birotteau is defrauded of his inheritance and hounded out of the lodgings. When aristocratic friends, the de Listomières, take up the cause, Troubert manipulates religious and political power via the central government to ensure that they abandon Birotteau. He carries his hatred for the wretched abbé to the point of breaking him completely; when Mme de Listomière dies, leaving him his second inheritance, Troubert brings pressure to bear on her son to have the abbé condemned for legacy-hunting. In all this Troubert works patiently, silently, through other people, using Sophie Gamard and discarding her, being only too happy at her death. His dangerous force fascinates Balzac while he condemns it. For, if society were organised in a way other than it is, the energies of Troubert might be harnessed to positive and altruistic ends.

The occult aspects of Balzac's thought contribute not only to the analysis of how individuals function in society, but also to the aesthetic problems of motivating physical description. He can use physical appearance and presence to communicate character traits and even to foreshadow events. The man of will reveals himself by his eyes, for example (cf Miss Wade in Dickens's *Little Dorrit* and Rosa Dartle in *David Copperfield*). So Vautrin, at the moment in *Père Goriot* when his true identity is unmasked, 'cast over Eugène that coldly fascinating look which certain particularly magnetic personalities have the power to project, and which, they say, has a calming effect on raving maniacs in madhouses'. For the magic fluid that constitutes the will is in part transmitted via the eyes. Such a fascination often plays a part in the hold that lovers have over one another. Magnetic attraction is the source of Etienne Lousteau's appeal for Dinah de la Baudraye in *La Muse du Département* and of Henri de Marsay's attractiveness to Paquita in *La Fille aux yeux d'or*. The cold Fedora, in *Peau de chagrin*, consciously prepares her gaze before it settles on a man 'as if something strange were happening within her, one might almost have said that a convulsion was taking place in those shining eyes of hers'. At moments of stress quite ordinary people can concentrate their energy into a glance, in order to command someone's attention. In *Une Fille d'Eve*, Marie de Vandenesse, desperate to contact Raoul Nathan at the opera as part of the plan to prevent him further compromising her, 'fixed on him that unwavering violent look by which the will flows forth from her eyes, as the luminous waves of light flood forth from the sun, and, according to the upholders of the magnetic theory, penetrates the person onto whom it is directed'.

The power of eyes, and the psychology it reveals, is within the control of the individual. The factors revealed by other elements of external appearance are often not so. For the theories of Lavater and Gall about head shape and similar features led Balzac to believe that the outer man betrayed the inner: 'The habits of life fashion the soul and the soul fashions the physiognomy', as he puts it in *Le Curé de Tours*. An extreme example of this is the description of Michu near the beginning of *Une ténébreuse affaire*. Michu is the faithful servant of the Simeuse twins, loyal royalists fighting for the émigré cause in the early days of the consulate. He secretly defends their financial interests against the *petits bourgeois* who have used the occasion of the Revolution to advance their own material position. The reward of his devotion will be to be implicated in a tortuous police plot against his young masters, and executed for a crime neither he nor they had any part in—the abduction of the Senator Malin, now possessor of the Simeuse estates. Michu bears the mark of this fate upon his brow from the beginning of the novel:

> The husband's appearance could up to a point have explained the two women's terror. The laws of physiognomy are exact, not only in their application to character, but even relative to the fatal course of an existence ... Yes, Destiny puts its mark upon the brows of those who are to die some violent death! Now this seal, visible to the eyes of the observer, was emprinted upon the expressive face of the man with the rifle. Small and stout, abrupt and agile as a monkey, though of a peaceful disposition, Michu had a white face, shot with blood, with the flattened features of a red-indian; red, curly hair gave it a sinister expression ... His hair, cut short at the front, and long at the sides and back, brought out, with its tawny red-ness, the full strangeness and ill-starred air of this physiognomy. The neck, short and fat, seemed to tempt the guillotine's blade.

Whatever we think of the ideas behind the description, as a device for arousing suspense in relation to a character it is effective.

There is, indeed, an irony in the gap which separates the view the modern reader will take of the balance between realism and the visionary in *La Comédie humaine* from the intentions and methods of its author. For the justification of much that seemed scientific to Balzac—the functioning of the individual character, the deterministic relationship between character and environment, the laws governing social change—now seems to be a largely aesthetic one, in that all these ideas give a unity and order to a potentially confused fictional world. The pursuit of money, its possession, its expenditure may seem to have little to do with psychological forces, but it is a highly acceptable symbol of power in a proto-capitalist society, and of the ruthless competition that such power generates. (Guy de Maupassant uses the same symbolism in a purely objective way in *Bel-ami*, without any of Balzac's theories but to exactly the same effect.) On the other hand, elements that Balzac introduced for largely aesthetic purposes are the very factors which add an air of reality to the world of the novels. The best example of this is probably the device of the recurrent character. Not until *Père Goriot* (1834) did Balzac begin the complex task of linking together all his novels by the reappearance of characters who would be in the foreground of one novel, the background of another. In new editions of works written prior to that date he replaced unnamed or even named characters with the names of characters from his new novels, gradually bringing the whole cycle of works into line. The immense advantage of this in terms of psychological realism is that knowledge of a character comes gradually, a hidden past is opened up, new facets are developed. As Balzac himself observed in the preface to *Une Fille d'Eve* (1839):

> ... that is how it is in the social world. In the middle of a salon you meet a man you have lost sight of for ten years; he is prime minister and a capitalist; when you knew him he didn't have a coat to his back ... then you go into a corner of the drawing-room, and there some delightful society raconteur fills you in, in half an hour, on the picturesque history of the ten or twenty years that you know nothing about ... Nothing in this world comes in a single block; it is all mosaic.

The novels—like Trollope's Barchester and Palliser cycles—become segments in time of a world that has been developing in between. Such devices as this give to *La Comédie humaine* the reality which Balzac sought to root in his own brand of scientism.

Although thirty years separated them, Zola was the first author after Balzac to attempt an analysis of society on anything like the same scale. But Zola, as we have seen, did not take entirely seriously the scientific theories he used. There are accordingly two quite separate ways in which his novels step outside the account of reality they purport to offer. One is through the element of social optimism, which becomes more facile the more overt it is—as in the post-Rougon-Macquart novels: the *Trois villes* (*Lourdes*, *Rome* and *Paris*) and the *Quatres Evangiles* (*Fécondité*, *Travail*, *Vérité*; the fourth, *Justice*, was unfinished at Zola's death). The second is through the element of poetry which suffuses Zola's vision, in his best writing at least. These qualities carry Zola out of the purely materialist category, and qualify him for a place among the idealists just as much as Fourier or Hugo. It is enough to contrast a Maupassant novel with one by Zola, if one really wants to bring out the difference between a pure naturalist and a visionary who grafts his symbols on to a naturalist base. In *Bel-ami* Maupassant describes the ruthless rise of a young ex-soldier, Georges Duroy, who possesses physical charm but few qualifications for anything; the setting is both the business world of journalism and the social world of the salon. It is the prototype for the genre of which John Braine's *Room at the Top* is a degenerate descendant. Maupassant's method in the novel is to rely exclusively upon a combination of acutely observed description and a determinist psychology which emerges from the facts of the action. He concerns himself with Duroy's love life, his ambitions, the forces in society itself which aid his progress. The only point where, in his selection of material, Maupassant could be accused of slanting the picture, is in his insistence on death and the awareness of death, which reaches a climax as Duroy stands beside his dying friend, Charles Forrestier:

> And suddenly Duroy remembered what Norbert de Varenne had been saying to him a few weeks before: 'For my own part I now sense death so close at hand that I often feel I want to stretch out an arm and push it away . . . I find it everywhere . . .' He had not understood at the time; now, as he looked at Forrestier, he could understand. And he was pierced by a feeling of agony, as if he had

become aware of hideous death within arm's reach, in the chair where this man lay gasping.

When Zola describes the career of a similar adventurer, Octave Mouret, in *Pot-bouille* and *Au Bonheur des Dames*, the centre of the two works is not the psychology of Octave but an impassioned denunciation of sexual indulgence and corruption as a poison sapping the structure of the middle classes. To convey this vision Zola relies not on the power of closely observed descriptions but on the incantatory return of the two great symbols: the block of flats 'like a whited sepulchre' in *Pot-bouille* and the great modern department store that gives its name to *Au Bonheur des Dames*.

One can, of course, go too far in playing down the scientific element. It was Taine who impressed on Zola the need to create in his novels a social panorama. Individual fortunes should be representative of wider social movements—political, economic and intellectual. What more natural than that, in putting this advice into practice, Zola should continue to adopt, as he had in his early novels, the principles of deterministic psychology which Taine himself had formulated. The twenty novels of the Rougon-Macquart cycle are designed to portray one particular '*moment*'— the France of the Second Empire—and as many different '*milieux*' as can be mustered—urban, rural, industrial—while exploring through the central characters the fortunes of one particular '*race*'—the thirty descendants, covering five generations, of Adelaide Fouque. The Rougon branch are the parvenus, descended from Pierre, whose face betrayed even in childhood 'the sly, cunning ambition, the insatiable need for satisfaction, the hardness of heart and hate-filled envy of a peasant's son whose mother's fortune and nervous temperament have made him into a bourgeois' (*La Fortune des Rougons*). The Macquarts are the illegitimate line, providing the lowest social strata that Zola explores. Thirdly, there are the Mourets, the cadet branch of the Macquarts, who maintain a higher social position than their cousins. All three branches of the family bear the taint of insanity (from old Adelaide) to which the Macquarts and Mourets add alcoholism (via Macquart, Adelaide's lover). The balance between exploration of the effects of heredity and of environment is deliberately altered to give variation to the novels in proportion as the breadth of vision changes from a wide-angle lens (eg, the working-class vistas of *L'Assommoir*) to a narrow one (eg, the private tragedy of a widow, the man she loves, and her little daughter, in *Une Page d'amour*). In the last novel of the series, *Le Docteur Pascal*, through the mouth of the eponymous hero, Zola analyses the family history and its medical implications, to round off the cycle. And what *Le Docteur Pascal* confirms is that even if Zola were not whole-hearted in his belief in the particular scientific theories he uses to motivate his work, his philosophy of life is a form of pure scientism. Through Pascal he proclaims a belief in material life and the duty of the individual to work for the inevitable social betterment which the expansion of knowledge will bring.

Modern critical opinion regards *L'Assommoir*, *Germinal* and *La Terre* as the greatest novels of the cycle, in that order; but in one major respect *L'Assommoir* is the least satisfactory of the three. For Zola is at his best when the determinism is environmental, and the more melodramatic aspects of the family tree are allowed to fade quietly into the background. Etienne Lantier in *Germinal* and Jean Macquart in *La Terre* provide the family link, but their role is very much that of the outsider in a community. The community itself—the economic oppression of the miners in *Germinal*, the obsessive relationship of the peasant to the land in *La Terre*—is the central theme of the novels. In *L'Assommoir* attention is divided between the analysis of working-class living conditions in Paris and the rise and fall of Gervaise Macquart. Her decline is brought about almost exclusively by an inborn tendency to alcoholism and fostered by a similar tendency in her husband. Nothing convinces us of the reality of the inherited trait. Gervaise is a hard-working woman struggling to bring up her two little boys after she is abandoned by her worthless lover, Lantier. As Henry James put it, she is 'richly human in her generosities and follies'. The man she marries, Coupeau, is equally a good man and a hard worker. In order to undermine this promising ménage, Zola—like Hardy in *Jude the Obscure*—resorts to a *coup de théâtre*. At the very moment when Gervaise is finally ready to set up her own little laundry, Coupeau falls from a roof on which he is working and is permanently crippled. Zola makes this a reason for alcoholism to assert itself, but the connexion does not seem a necessary one. The stroke of fate is authorial and not rationally developed, which has the unhappy effect of making the novel fall apart in the centre. Nevertheless there is immense power in the descriptions of life in this forgotten quarter of Paris, close to the Gare du Nord, and immense pathos in the gradual decline of Gervaise as she loses the strength and motivation to struggle against a wastrel husband, takes comfort in drink and loses everything in life for which she had fought so hard.

In *Germinal* the fatality is inherent in the relentless world of the mining community, on which the first eleven chapters dwell. As the impressions of a succession of characters reveal, overwork, poverty and inhuman working conditions act as constraints on the miners and their families, and show the mindless animality of their psychology to be the tragic product of a particular economic system. The pathos of this world is deepened by the small touches of the quiet virtues which survive: Catherine Maheu, timidly reappearing in the family house for the first time since she went to live with Chaval, has bought coffee and sugar from her meagre savings for her little brothers and sisters; and Maheu insists that the little ones should have a share in the piece of meat his wife has managed to get for him:

> But the smell of the meat had made Lénore and Henri lift their heads, as they played on the ground at drawing little streams with the water. Both of them came and stood by their father, the little boy in front. Their eyes followed each piece, watched, full of

93

hope, as it left the plate, and, with consternation saw it engulfed into the mouth. Eventually their father noticed the air of greed which made them pale and wet their lips.

'Have the children had any?' he asked. And, as his wife hesitated: 'You know I don't like that sort of unfairness. It makes me lose my appetite to see them here, around me, begging for a piece.'
... He sat Lénore on his left thigh, Henri on his right; then he finished up the pork brawn, sharing it out into a little snack with them. Each had their ration, he cut little pieces for them. The children, in their delight, ate ravenously.

When Zola has established the physical and psychological reality of the community, he is able to use it as a single 'actor' in its own right, responding in a unified way to various stimuli—a terrifying study in mass psychology. The centre of the book is a long dramatic conflict between the miners, who are driven to strike by the threat of a reduction in their bread-line standard of living, and the middle-class management, who are almost helpless as the agents of the company and its remote shareholders. The first high point is the explosion of the starving mob which wrecks machinery —contrast the similar scene in Charlotte Brontë's *Shirley*—and murders the local grocer who has been exploiting the people for so long and now refuses them credit. The second is the clash with the soldiers sent in to protect strike-breaking immigrant labour. And the third is the flooding of the pit by act of sabotage after the miners have been forced into submission and have returned to work. Each of these events grows naturally out of the situation, so that the whole book is a relentless development from a given premise.

So far, then, we can see in Zola a writer of meticulous materialism, confining himself to the portraiture of things as they are. He has successfully avoided the danger of using realistic presentation to clothe abnormal and improbable subjects—a danger which dogged so many novels of social investigation, notably those of the Goncourt brothers. But *Germinal* and, less obviously, *L'Assommoir* do not rely for artistic success on the probability of their physical and psychological portraits. They skilfully manipulate the reader's emotions by symbolism. The central symbol in *Germinal* is that of the mine, frequently described in animal terms as a devourer of men, a living hell. The emotional force of the novel is greatly enhanced by this kind of poetic device. And the end of the book balances hell by the promise of paradise in the symbol of germination, the seeds of the revolution through which the working class shall rightfully inherit the earth. As Etienne walks away from the mine for ever, he feels his erstwhile comrades mining away deep down below, and the rebirth of spring in the surface world becomes united in his mind with the birth of their future:

All around seeds were swelling, growing, cracking the surface of the plain, tormented by a desire for heat and light. Sap overflowed in a fountain of whispering voices, the sound of plants sprouting up spread out in a huge kiss. Again and again, more and more distinctly, as if they had come closer to the surface of the ground, his comrades were tapping. In the fiery rays of the heavenly orb, on this youthful morning, the countryside was pregnant with this distant sound. Men were growing, a black army of revenge, slowly germinating in the furrows, growing for the harvest of future centuries, and whose sprouting up would soon burst through the face of the earth.

This type of lyrical evocation of natural forces provides the whole theme of *La Terre*, where the land takes over the symbolic role played by the mine in *Germinal*. The friar Archangias, in *La Faute de l'abbé Mouret*, remarks contemptuously of the villagers: 'they'ld be ready to fornicate with their plots of land, they love them so much'. In *La Terre* this idea is taken up and developed into an overwhelming evocation of the passionate clinging to the land which characterises the peasantry, an erotic and jealous passion that divides family from family and brother from brother. At the opening of the book old Fouan reluctantly decides to give up the cultivation of his farm and distribute it between his two sons and his daughter. The decision costs him a good deal:

He had loved the earth like a woman who kills and for whom murder is done. Not wife, children anybody, anything human meant the same as the earth! And here he was, grown old, and forced to yield his mistress up to his sons...

Like King Lear—whom Zola had much in mind during the writing of the novel—Fouan lives to regret his trust in filial affection. The narrative of the novel recounts the family divisions caused by the ownership and prospective ownership of land, and the difference in attitude to the earth between the outsider, Jean Macquart, and those who are born to it. Eventually, Jean withdraws from a life in which he cannot fully share, his wife having been murdered by her sister and Buteau, Fouan's younger son, to whom she is married. The melodramatic narrative is really secondary to the novel's main function, which is to convey the experience of nature as an independent force and the effect that exposure to raw nature has on man. The cycle of the seasons, the recurrent images of the sea—that symbol of infinity—in descriptions of the Beauce landscape, the pictures of seed-sowing that open and close the novel, remind one that the individual dies but man lives on.

L'Assommoir, *Germinal* and *La Terre* undoubtedly present a materialist view of the universe. Whether they offer a scientific account of life as it was at that period is a different matter. Zola moves beyond a determinist psychology when our understanding of human nature ceases to derive from the action of the novel and is emotionally stimulated by poetic symbols, such as the mine or the landscape. Even in *La Conquête de Plassans*, perhaps Zola's most truly naturalist novel—a factual account of the political conversion of a small provincial town to the cause of Louis-Napoleon—the clinical description of insanity in François Mouret and of religious mania in his wife Marthe, and the wider vista of family madness which it opens up, suggests forces at work that defy rational comprehension. If we go to the other end of the scale, to one of Zola's least naturalistic works, *La Faute de l'Abbé Mouret*, this inherent tendency to poeticise is revealed as a truly visionary approach to the understanding of life. The novel is a portrait of what Zola sees as a struggle between religion and life, a theme he will take up in a very different way in *Le Rêve* and again in *Lourdes*. A comparison of the three novels shows the ambivalence of his feelings towards religion. In *Lourdes* he fiercely attacks Catholicism as a delusion which is preventing the advance of scientism and hence the natural evolution of human progress. In *Le Rêve*—like Flaubert in *Trois contes*, especially 'A Simple Heart'—he seems to suggest that, though religion is a deception, it can offer a form of happiness not open to the non-believer. The innocent and deeply pious Angélique—who has all the more saccharine qualities of Dickens's Little Nell but an intensity and strength of character more reminiscent of Flaubert's Saint Julien—dies on the cathedral steps the moment after her marriage: 'She tottered . . . With a last effort she raised herself up. She brought her mouth against Felicien's mouth. And in the moment of that kiss, she died.' In his plans for the novel, the author noted: 'She dies fulfilled, in ecstasy, exalted by the realisation of her dream, at the very moment where she is entering upon reality.' Angélique may, like Emma Bovary, have distorted her personality by contact with literature, in her case the medieval *Golden Book*, with its tales of saints and miracles; but, unlike Emma, she dies 'at the summit of her happiness . . . at the breath of a little kiss'.

La Faute de l'Abbé Mouret presents the reverse of the medal; indeed *Le Rêve* was written as a pendant to it, so that Zola could express himself more clearly on the religious issue. The three sections of the novel are symmetrically structured. In the first, the young Abbé Mouret, an unworldly priest particularly attached to the cult of the Immaculate Conception of Our Lady, goes about his duties in a parish notable for its debased sensuality. The abbé's obsession with spiritual, and consequently physical, purity is the central theme, put psychologically into perspective by a review of his childhood, and coming to a climax in the fevered self-immolation of his moonlight prayer to the Virgin to rid him of earthly taints: 'O Mary, vase of election, castrate the humanity in me, make me a eunuch among men so that you may yield up to me without fear the treasure of your virginity'. The abbé's search for perfect purity is counterpointed not only by village lust but also by the earthy simplicity of his half-witted sister, Désirée, who lives very close to the farmyard animals she tends and loves. Behind the abbé stands the possessed figure of Brother Archangias, the fanatical and foul-mouthed reviler of the things of the flesh.

In the second section, it emerges that the abbé, now known only by his christian name, Serge, has suffered an attack of brain-fever, and consequent amnesia, as a result of the intensity of his religious passions. He has been brought by his physician uncle—eventually to be the eponymous hero of *Le Docteur Pascal*—to a neglected walled estate, where he is looked after by Albine, the wild young daughter of the eccentric lodge-keeper. Serge experiences a physical and mental rebirth closely associated with the gradual development of his relationship with Albine. Hard on the consummation of their love comes the moment, partly engineered by Archangias, when Serge regains the memory of his priesthood, and renounces Albine and the idyllic world in which they have learned to love one another.

The final section shows the abbé consciously repressing the physical in himself, just as in the first part he had unconsciously repressed it. The statuette of the Immaculate Conception in his room is now replaced by a great black crucifix, his love for Our Lady by the masochist cult of the agonies of Our Lord. In the subsequent struggle it is Albine who is the loser, for, though Serge is eventually willing to return to her, religion has achieved the emasculation for which he once so earnestly prayed. She commits suicide, leaving the abbé to face the world, and himself, alone.

The powerful conflict between spirituality and sensuality is presented in a series of complex symbols which do not allow of an easy resolution as far as the allocation of right and wrong are concerned. At times the symbols even run counter to any logic, as when Albine is described as white-skinned, to stress the purity embodied in her name, though she is a child of the sun; or as when Serge's body hair, which flourishes while he is in the park, disappears when he resumes the 'feminine' garb of the priesthood. The central section of the book is one continuous image, a vast inversion of the Genesis myth. The name of the park is Le Paradou—Paradise—and the process by which Serge regains his health is a 'creation'. First the garden is created, as one moves from the darkness of Serge's room and the rain outside to the birth of light and springtime. When eventually Albine gets her patient into the garden, he awakens, from his mental sleep, as a new Adam. Not only is stress put on his rebirth but Albine becomes the Eve created from his inmost self:

'Who are you? Where do you come from? What are you doing at my side?'

She was still smiling, delighted to see him wakening like this. Then he seemed to remember; he went on, with a gesture of happiness and confidence: 'I know you are my love, you come from my flesh, you are waiting for me to take you into my arms, for us to become no more than one . . . I dreamed of you. You were within my breast, and I gave you my blood, my muscles, my bones . . . And I woke up when you came forth from my body.'

The garden, their paradise, embraces a whole world of its own, with every sort of vegetation and animal life. Zola constantly portrays it as an infinite, living force in its own right, particularly through his use of sea metaphors:

A sea of greenery, in front, to right, to left, everywhere. A sea whose waves of foliage rose and fell right away to the horizon, unbroken by any house, or stretch of wall, or dusty road. A sea that was empty, virgin, sacred, unfolding its wild sweetness in the innocence of solitude.

The lovers gradually explore this world, and each stage of their exploration, developing a new stage of their relationship, involves a new natural symbol. So, while their love is at its innocent and childlike beginning, and they are exploring the riot of flowers in the garden, it is among the lilies, traditional emblem of purity (and perhaps of death), that they come to rest:

> They had come from the roses through all the flowers to the lilies. The lilies offered them a refuge of innocence, after their lovers' walk, amid the ardent solicitation of the sweet honeysuckles, the musky violets, the verbena with its scent as fresh as a kiss . . . And there they stayed, like two child lovers, sovereignly chaste, as though at the centre of a tower of purity, an unassailable ivory tower.

Gradually they move from this pre-pubic stage into a period of adolescent frustration, conveyed by a part of the garden containing 'sinister' plants—rue, valerian, hemlock, belladonna—towards physical fulfilment. This growth of sexual awareness is also connected with the search for a tree—a tree of knowledge—which Albine senses to be the most perfect part of the garden and yet, obscurely, to be forbidden. The eventual discovery of the tree and their sexual union comes not just as the natural fulfilment of their private relationship but as a mystical moment when the whole world explodes into an erotic yet creative frenzy:

> From the most distant corners, from the patches of sunlight, from the hollows of shadow, an animal odour rose, warm with the universal rutting. All this pullulating life had the thrill of childbirth running through it. Beneath every leaf an insect was conceiving; in every tuft of grass a family was growing; flies in the air, clinging to one another, could not wait to come to rest in order to fertilise each other. The fragments of invisible life which people matter, the very atoms of matter themselves, imparted a voluptuous rocking to the ground making the whole park one enormous act of fornication.
>
> Then Albine and Serge knew. He said nothing; he enfolded her ever closer in his arms. The destiny of procreation surrounded them. They yielded to the demands of the garden. It was the tree

which whispered into Albine's ear what mothers whisper in the
ears of brides on their wedding nights.

Albine gave herself. Serge possessed her.

And the whole garden drowned itself, with the couple, in a last
cry of passion.

The destruction of the idyll is brought about by Archangias, the
emissary of God (the name suggests archangel); he has reopened
a breach in the park wall, through which Serge sees the 'real'
world of his parish and hears the fateful call of the angelus bells.
It is God who drags Serge from paradise, out of spite against the
perfection of the natural world.

The symbolism, however, is not as straightforward as that. In
Zola's work the association of sexuality always has overtones of
violence and corruption, if the relationship is not a deliberately
procreative one; nowhere more so than in *La Curée*, where the
world-weary Renée and her depraved young stepson, Maxime,
indulge their lusts in a garden almost as luxuriant as Le Paradou.
If the natural union achieved by Serge and Albine avoids this
corruption, it is because of the special nature of the park itself. Le
Paradou is an image of an ideal world, where a reborn human
nature could flourish. Outside its walls, sexuality is divided between the debased and loveless life of the village, whose sterility is
typified in the death of promiscuous Rosalie's baby, and the
mindless cycle of 'nature red in tooth and claw', represented by
Désirée—the forerunner of Zulma in Jean Giono's *Que ma joie
demeure*. Undoubtedly Serge's religion is for Zola a cruel illusion,
and the sickening Brother Archangias is the prototype of the
repulsive priests who disfigure the pages of his last completed
novel, *Vérité*. But the perfect accord of the lovers and nature in its
full mystical pantheism is only a wistful vision, with nothing to
suggest that it could be compatible with human nature and society
as we know them.

The visionary side of Zola's work is, then, sufficiently in evidence in the Rougon-Macquart cycle for it to be no surprise when

it comes to the fore in the later novels. What had previously been a discreet insistence that the material perfecting of the world could and would take place, however hopeless things might seem in the present, becomes, in the *Quatres Evangiles* especially, overt preaching of a religion of science, a kind of technological socialism. Bertheroy, the author's spokesman in *Paris*, proclaims in the last chapter:

> Only science is revolutionary; it is the only force which, above petty political events, above the vain agitation of sectarians and the ambitious, is working for the humanity of tomorrow, preparing its truth, its justice, its peace.

Fécondité preaches the—rather unscientific— virtues of large families and the vices of birth control. In *Travail*, the dream is of a society where the work will all be done by machines and the people left free to improve their minds. Zola uses the occasion to preach a brand of Fourierism and predict the growth of a model society. The last completed novel, *Vérité*, is a transposition of the events of the Dreyfus case (see p 197) into a context that permits a violent denunciation of Christianity in general and of Catholicism in particular, coupled with proposals for the improvement of primary education. All these works are moralistic tracts in which the reader is simply directed to accept what Henry James called 'the convention of the blameless being, the thoroughly "scientific" creature possessed impeccably of all truth and serving as the mouthpiece of it and of the author's highest commonplaces'. James ('Emile Zola' in *Atlantic Monthly*, 1903) places these later novels in the literary tradition to which they rightly belong:

> Marc in *Vérité*, Pierre Froment in *Lourdes* and in *Rome*, the wondrous representatives of the principle of reproduction in *Fécondité* ... such figures show us the reasonable and the good not merely in the white light of the old George Sand novel and its improved moralities; but almost in that of our childhood's nursery and schoolroom, that of the moral tale of Miss Edgeworth and Mr Thomas Day.

Zola in old age, like Comte, departed farther and farther from the principles of science in the name of science, and replaced detached analysis of what is with impassioned prescription of what should be. This idealist tendency is only acceptable when disguised in the type of poetic symbolism used in *La Terre* or *La Faute de l'Abbé Mouret* for the ideas betray how naïve and, by the end, how old-fashioned Zola was as a thinker.

CONCLUSIONS

What emerges from a comparison of French idealists and materialists from Chateaubriand to Zola is that the great division of the age is not between idealists and materialists at all but between two sorts of idealists. Most thinkers were profoundly dissatisfied with the world as it was. The question was: could the moral improvement of man be derived from his material progress or should he look to values outside material existence? In Victorian England there was no difficulty in accepting both paths, as one finds in the sentimental optimism of Browning, for example. In France, those who believed that science was the touchstone of reality envisaged the perfectability of human society on an exclusively material level. Those who believed that science gave an inadequate account of life looked to God, or to pantheism or to other metaphysical abstractions, to provide the guarantee of a new morality and a goal towards which man could aim. Both these groups are in that sense idealists. To emphasise this, I have deliberately broken the common groupings, which would classify Stendhal and Flaubert as rationalists or Dumas the younger as an idealist. Though he deals in moral abstracts, Dumas is ultimately concerned with purely material ends; though they analyse the world in terms of material phenomena, Stendhal and Flaubert value illusions. Thus, the emotional religiosity of the earlier part of the century and the rational scientism of the central and later part spring from the same earnest desire for stability, happiness and progress towards perfection, but the two types of writer choose fundamentally different approaches to its attainment.

Of course, a limited number of writers, like Augier, were more or less satisfied with life as it was. A rather more substantial number were driven into a state of philosophical pessimism by the apparent pointlessness of pursuing any ideal within the framework of society; some of them (see p 160), including Flaubert and Leconte de Lisle, were attracted to the possibility that art in itself could provide a sufficient ideal. But the first substantial reorientation of nineteenth-century thought occurred with the fundamental questioning of the assumption that the data offered by our senses are necessarily reliable. Although a complete philosophical exposition of an alternative doctrine had to wait until Henri Bergson (1859–1941), the problem had been raised throughout the period we have been considering, particularly by poets. The tension between illusion and reality was to be matched by the conflicting claims of the subjective eye and the objective world.

The question poses itself: was there any relation between these intellectual and cultural developments and the state of French society from the Consulate to the beginning of the Third Republic? If the precariousness of life in the aftermath of the Revolution was in part responsible for the original crises of values, how far were ensuing social changes responsible for the development of that crisis and of the two types of idealism which were offered as solutions? The period 1800–52 is not noted for its political stability. The Consulate became an empire, the Bourbons returned, were chased out again by Napoleon, and finally restored in 1815. Throughout that period France was on a war footing, and the pursuit of military glory proved as incompatible with economic progress or social stability as had been the political confusions of the Revolution itself. The fifteen years of the Bourbon restoration were equally stultifying in their effect. Between 1815 and 1830 the population of France increased by nearly $2\frac{1}{2}$ million, but the increase was not matched by significant rises in agricultural or industrial productivity. Consequently the economic condition of the lower classes actually deteriorated. As for higher social strata, the middle-class felt intense resentment at the reappearance of a nobility which seemed to feel that the *ancien régime* had never ceased to exist. It was a period, too, of intellectual claustrophobia, both because of the substantial censorship exercised under both Empire and Restoration, and because of the desire common to Napoleon, Louis XVIII and Charles X to aid the spurious air of continuity between pre- and post-revolutionary society by en-couraging a cultural 'continuity' that was in fact a cultural revival. The mummified preservation of neo-classical tragedy is a case in point. So that, of the whole period 1800-30, it can fairly be said that nothing happened to encourage confidence in the ability of society to solve any of its pressing intellectual or social prob-lems at a material level. It is precisely at this period that the greatest initial impetus towards metaphysical systems and the reinstatement of non-rational values can be traced.

The July monarchy represented an ostensible political change. Yet it was not a change to please the intellectuals. It was the turn of the *bourgeoisie* to exploit power for their own ends, and they were no more interested in rectifying the comparative economic backwardness of the country than their predecessors had been. The gap between rich and poor widened and became more ob-vious, as the urban centres swelled without being able to provide a living for their increased population. It was, in other words, a régime of vested material interests. In intellectual circles it was plain that problems of social inequality were substantially moral problems too. Even a thinker so congenitally feeble as poor George Sand could see this. It is the very core of her revolt against society in those novels compounded from a jumble of absurd utopian and spiritualist theories, eg *Consuelo*; it underlies such ludicrous idealisations of the peasantry as *Petite Fadette* or *François le Champi*. Even in her early novels, with their grotesquely melodramatic stylisations of adultery at its most clichéd, *Indiana* or *Jacques* (forerunners of the 'hot passion and dramatic suicide' school of twentieth-century pulp novel), the moral corrosion effected by the social structure is constantly felt as a primary cause of individual inadequacy.

This was not the only factor alienating intellectuals from their political environment. The material self-satisfaction of the ruling clique was matched by its cultural philistinism. When ideas are not valued in the service of society, they easily find their way into opposition to it. Hence the 1830s and 1840s are a period of intellectual revolt *par excellence*, culminating in the Second Republic—the moment when it seemed that political idealism, whether tied to metaphysical systems or positivist principles, had its chance of genuinely affecting the course of society. In the event, of course, the republic was a fiasco. The middle-classes proved exceptionally efficient at keeping political and economic power in their own hands. The economic crisis intensified, unemployment rose, starvation among the urban proletariat became a serious problem. As a result, class hatred reached a new pitch. The chaos of the Revolution seemed to have taught men very little.

The coup d'état of 1851, and the formal establishment of the Second Empire in the following year, marked the beginning of a genuine development, at least as far as economic policy was concerned. Louis-Napoleon was attracted by Saint-Simonian ideas on the need for economic expansion and the primacy of technocrats in society. The society which resulted was certainly more stable but no more equal, although the extremes of poverty were mitigated. With the growth of wealth, the accent on material success as the sole end worthy in itself completed that process of alienation which the intellectuals had felt under Louis-Philippe. For half a century France had had no fixed spiritual values. Now it was made clear that none were required. The natural response from the intellectual community was for it to turn its back on bourgeois pragmatism and the philistinism for which it was held responsible. Even the most materialist thinkers tended to temper their philosophies with respect for the claims of non-rational phenomena in reaction against the popular debasement of the rationalist position. Intellectual and governmental circles were mutually exclusive, a trend established under the July monarchy. Indeed, the nearest thing to culture identifiable with establishment circles were the comic operettas of Offenbach, which for all their many virtues must be accounted a fairly narrow species of art. The 'alternative society' was responsible for what artistic success and intellectual progress existed in the France of the 1850–70 epoque. Despite the efforts of the newly created minister of fine arts under the so-called 'Liberal Empire' (1870–1) to end the official contempt for taste and intelligence, it was not until the immense re-orientation of both political and intellectual society occasioned by the Dreyfus affair that the situation really began to change.

CHAPTER 3

Subjective Reality

Throughout nineteenth-century French literature, a consistent feature is a fascination with the nature and powers of the self. There is some basis for this in the philosophical preoccupations of the period. In the previous century Jean-Jacques Rousseau in his *Confessions* (1764–70) and *Rêveries d'un promeneur solitaire* (1776–8) had already articulated the revolt of many of his contemporaries against that intellectual delight in systems which had reduced the status of the individual in society to that of cog in a massive machine. He felt that the pressure of social conformism had distorted the individual's personality, making him less self-sufficient and therefore more aggressive in his dealings with his fellows. Rousseau's own preoccupations were with ways in which new social institutions could be developed that would not pervert the qualities of 'natural' man. But the facet of his writing which most impressed subsequent generations was his analysis of his inner self, particularly of his sense of otherness; 'I am not made like any man that I have seen; I venture to think I am not made like any man who exists. If I am no better, I am at least different.' This awareness of uniqueness is at the same time closely bound up with doubts about the identity of both self and others, and with a sense of the paramount importance of his own perceptions, feelings and imagination as tools for reaching conclusions on these problems of the inner and outer worlds. Though Rousseau saw reason as a necessary addition to the other three 'tools' in creating the inner voice that would guide him on the path to human progress, it is a short step from his sense of alienation and his rejection of contemporary reliance on intellect to the belief that it is only the experiences undergone by the individual self which are meaningful, and that all rational activity distorts our apprehension of the true nature of the world around us. It was a step many writers of the nineteenth century proved eager to take.

It is nonetheless difficult to trace any clear philosophical development of ideas about the self until quite late on in the nineteenth century. This seems curious when we remember that Mme de Staël in *De l'Allemagne* (1810) was already popularising the views of those German philosophers who, together with their successors, were to influence French poets from Nerval to Mallarmé. In the first seven chapters of part 3 of *De l'Allemagne*—after a few thoughts on the importance of philosophy within a given culture and a critique of the materialism of recent English and French philosophers—Mme de Staël examines in turn the principal tenets of Leibniz, Kant, Fichte, and Schelling, together with a number of others considered in rather less detail. Of the two qualities which she constantly praises in these thinkers, the first, as one might expect, is the importance they give to the emotions; the second is the value they place upon the self:

> The really admirable aspect of German philosophy is the self-analysis which it obliges us to make. It goes back to the origins of the will. to that unknown spring whence flows the stream of our life. And it is by that penetration into the most intimate secrets of pain and faith that it enlightens and strengthens us.

Fichte, whom she met, perhaps interested her most, though she rightly sees him as a lesser thinker than Kant. Fichte believed that the existence and form of the outer world is dependent on the subjective experience of each individual. In other words, a table exists and has its particular form only because one chooses to see it so—Bertrand Russell's example when discussing this tenet in *The Problems of Philosophy*. This concept revolutionised the role of the creative imagination, for it left the poet free to conjure up from his inner perceptions a world quite different from the 'deceptive' one of commonsense material surfaces. But it is not this aspect of Fichte that interested Mme de Staël so much as the implications of his philosophy for the understanding of the self:

> The chief merit of Fichte's philosophy is the incredible strength of concentration that it supposes. For not content with referring everything to man's inner existence, to that self which is the basis for everything, he goes so far as to distinguish within that self a transient element and a durable element. In truth, when you reflect upon the workings of your understanding, you have the impression of being a spectator of your own thought-processes, of watching your thought pass as though it were a wave, while that part of you that is watching is immutable. Those who combine a passionate character with great powers of observation often have the experience of watching themselves suffer, and feeling within themselves a being who is above its own suffering, who watches it and blames it or sympathises with it in turns.
>
> Continual changes are brought about within us by the external circumstances of our lives, and yet we retain the sense of our own identity. What testifies to this identity, if not the unchanging element within the self, which sees that part of the self which is modified by external impressions pass before its seat of judgement?

In purely literary spheres such ideas were to be influential. The problem of identity is central, for example, to the heroes of Romantic drama such as Musset's *Lorenzaccio*. In a more mystical form it occurs in Théophile Gautier's poems on metamorphosis and sexual duality, in his short stories and in his novel, *Mademoiselle de Maupin*. Similarly the particular question of the relation between the ephemeral and the constant within the self is reflected in both subject and form of Benjamin Constant's *Adolphe*. Yet no systematic philosophical interest was shown by contemporary thinkers. There are a number of possible reasons for this. For almost half a century the established form of French philosophy was eclecticism, whose predominantly metaphysical concerns put it above issues of merely psychological importance. It was succeeded by positivism, which was hostile both to the claims of the individual to be in any significant sense different from his fellows and to the idea that the non-rational processes, such as intuition, could yield significant truths not attainable by scientific means. Not until Henri Bergson (1859–1941) were non-rational processes incorporated into a radically new philosophical exposition of the nature of reality. At the same time the leaders of the Romantic movement in France—Lamartine, Musset, Hugo—unlike their German counterparts showed themselves more interested in formal reform—the rejection of traditional restraints in versification and in the structure of plays—than in exploring new theories of perception. So that it was left to individuals, often poets, to introduce new evaluations of the nature and role of the self to the French public. Consequently the ideas were fragmented, individually interpreted or incorporated into new aesthetic theories rather than presented for their own sake or developed as philosophical issues *per se*. Invaluable to the individual writer, they did not gain general currency.

Despite this fragmentation the nature of the problems raised may be clarified as generally falling under four headings:

a How valid is the evidence of our senses? Do we have reliable evidence of anything outside ourselves?
b If we cannot know the world around us, can we still attain knowledge of universals by exploring our own minds?
c What is the importance of imagination and intuition in our knowledge of ourselves, the world around us, and whatever lies beyond that?
d How can we establish our own identity, and what are the problems of self-knowledge?

These questions and a variety of answers offered to them by

foreign philosophers were in the minds of many writers from the 1830s onwards.

Self as subject

It is a commonplace that French Romantic poets devoted much energy to revealing and analysing their own feelings and experiences. But interest in the self went beyond this superficial egoism. A more authentic form of self-analysis is to be found in certain early prose works. Senancour in *Oberman* (1804) proclaims that 'a man's real life is within him', but takes the view that, in the determination of who or what he is, a man cannot consider himself in total isolation: 'An isolated being is never perfect; his existence is incomplete'. As Matthew Arnold succinctly puts it in his notes to his poem 'Stanzas in memory of the author of Obermann':

> Though *Obermann*, a collection of letters from Switzerland treating almost entirely of nature and of the human soul, may be called a work of sentiment, Senancour has a gravity and severity which distinguish him from all other writers of the sentimental school. The world is with him in his solitude far less than it is with them; of all writers he is the most perfectly isolated and the least attitudinising . . . The stir of all the main forces by which modern life is and has been impelled lives in the letters of *Obermann*; the dissolving agencies of the eighteenth century, the fiery storm of the French Revolution, the first faint promise and dawn of that new world which our own time is but now more fully bringing to light—all these are to be felt, almost to be touched there.

There are in *Oberman* no definitive answers to the problem of knowledge, but there is a clear assertion of the relationship between the problems of the individual and those of his environment and epoque.

Senancour also touches upon the issue raised by Chateaubriand in his *Mémoires d'Outre-Tombe*—that of the continuity of the self.

Certain introspective novelists of the period, Sainte-Beuve in *Volupté* (1834) and Fromentin in *Dominique* (1863), pragmatically assume the consistency of the human personality. Senancour at least recognises the importance of inconsistency within an individual's experience. Chateaubriand considers the significance of such inconsistency at a rather deeper level: 'If man did but confine his changes to change of place! But his life and his heart must be always changing too'. In *Mémoires d'Outre-Tombe* he constantly finds that his personality is subject to the law of flux. Familiar and once important objects, events or places lose their value in a different temporal context: 'Dieppe is empty of my self; it was another *me*, a self of days long gone by, who once inhabited this place, and this self has passed, for our past dies before we do.'

Yet the attempt to come to terms with this discontinuity of the self without stepping outside the psychological limits of the self —though it is implicit, as will be seen, in Constant's *Adolphe*, only became important at the end of the century, in the work of André Gide and later of Marcel Proust. Instead, certain writers, notably Gautier, explore the idea that the discontinuity can be transcended on a supernatural plane. Charles Nodier (1780–1844), with *Smarra* (1821), *Trilby* (1822) and *La Fée aux miettes* (1832), had already linked such relevant issues as the nature of dreams and the definition of sanity with the supernatural in the form of popular Gothic fantasy. But his malignant sprites do not have the symbolic value of, say, Christina Rossetti's 'Goblin Market'. He plainly uses the supernatural as a literary device. Gautier in some of his *Contes fantastiques* (1831–52) and in *Spirite* (1865) studies the relation of the self and the supernatural in a much more serious fashion. He suggests that the conscious mind conceals a mysterious alternative reality in which conventional time and distance cease to apply, allowing man not only to be coherent with earlier states of his own self but also to commune with other souls. In *Arria Marcella* the hero Octavien has a great potential love that he cannot realise in the context of physical reality. On a visit to

Pompeii he becomes fascinated with the imprint of a female body on a piece of lava. The power of his desire literally brings to life the classical world to which the woman, Arria Marcella, belonged. This idea, rather than being an excuse for an exotic tale, is developed at some length for its own sake, as when Gautier explains:

> In fact, nothing dies, everything exists eternally: no force can annihilate what once has been. Every action, every word, every form, every thought dropped into the universal ocean of things produces ripples in it that spread ever outward to the shores of eternity. The material form only disappears for vulgar eyes; the spectres which detach themselves from that form people the infinite ... Some passionate and powerful minds have been able to bring back for themselves ages apparently lost in time, and to resurrect people dead to everybody.

However, though Octavien's desire momentarily brings to life the vanished world of Pompeii and the exotic figure of the Roman courtesan, he is denied the consummation of his passion and returns to a discontented and distracted life in the present: Gautier sardonically marries him off to a very practical Englishwoman called Ellen.

This frustration of union is significant. It occurs in many of Gautier's stories, is implicit in some of his poems and essential to his finest novel, *Mademoiselle de Maupin* (1835–6), where the sexual ambiguities of Shakespeare's *As You Like It* are used to symbolise the self yearning for a completion in love which is not attainable because reality is never totally transcended. Sometimes no physical relationship is achieved, as in *Arria Marcella*; sometimes the physical relationship, though attained, cannot be maintained, as in *Mademoiselle de Maupin*. But fulfilment of the self and full communion with another can only be achieved by going beyond physical urges to a mystic spiritual union. This occurs in only one of Gautier's works: the late novella, *Spirite*. Guy de Malivert, insensible to the normal violence of human passion, is encouraged by the Baron de Féroë, a young Swedish disciple of

Swedenborg, to take an interest in the occult. As a result, he makes contact with Spirite, the disembodied soul of Lavinia d'Aufideni, who unknown to him died of unrequited love for him. From the moment when Spirite first manifests herself to him as a reflection in his mirror, Malivert experiences 'that immaterial desire, that winged volition to which the glimpse of an angel gives birth'. Spirite seeks gradually to wean Malivert away from the physical world and to purify him so that their souls can unite. Malivert overcomes the tensions between his physical desire for the female form in which Spirite manifests herself and the angelic abstract that is her real essence. His physical body is assassinated on a visit to Greece, but from the evidence of an eyewitness, and the final vision of the united souls vouchsafed to the Baron de Féroë, Malivert's soul achieves the longed-for union. A substantial portion of this tale is given over to the exposition of mystical doctrines, notably in the description by Spirite of the nature of the self as it is preserved in the after-life. The message, if that is the right term, is of the bliss, transcending all physical experience, which is afforded by the blending of two souls into one eternal essence. For, as Spirite tells Malivert when she appears to him as he is enjoying the intense beauty of a night voyage across the Aegean:

> If you let fall to the very bottom of you, as though to the depths of still waters, the gross and impure human clay ... we shall be guaranteed to taste in eternal union the calm intoxication of divine love, that love which knows no intermittence, no weakening, no weariness, and whose flame would melt suns like grains of myrrh upon the fire. We shall be unity in duality, self in the non-self, motion in repose, desire in fulfilment, freshness in fire.

Malivert will achieve the ultimate harmony, denied to Louis Lambert in Balzac's novel of that name, by a process of gradual purification similar to that undergone by the androgynous Séraphita-Séraphitus in Balzac's *Séraphita*. The problems of the self, for Gautier, can only be solved by abandoning the call of reality altogether and looking to the mysterious possibilities of the world beyond.

The idea that happiness lies in the exclusion of the physical world and the attainment of a new sphere accessible only to the self is not one only cultivated by writers interested in the fantastic. Its greatest exponent among 'realists' is Flaubert, whose *Three Tales* has as its central and underlying image that of man shedding his contacts with society in the pursuit, conscious or not, of sainthood. The three stories are very different in matter, each relating superficially to one of Flaubert's novels. The first, 'A Simple Heart', is set, like *Madame Bovary* and *Education sentimentale*, in mid-nineteenth-century France. It describes the uneventful life of a peasant, Felicity, from girlhood to decrepit old age and death. The second, 'The Legend of Saint Julian the Hospitaler', is, like *La Tentation de St Antoine*, an apparently straight-faced retelling of a Christian legend. The third, 'Hérodias', takes place, like *Salammbô*, in antiquity, and shows Herod Antipas, the events leading to the famous dance of Salome, and the death of John the Baptist. The differences in subject are, however, less significant than the unity of meaning. In 'A Simple Heart' we witness the stripping bare of a human soul. In youth Felicity has her one love affair thwarted; the object of her affections, Theodore, prefers to marry a rich old woman who can buy him out of conscription into the army. When Felicity's would-be lover is taken away, she goes into the service of Mme Aubain. Each person to whom she gives herself willingly is taken away from her: Mme Aubain's children, Paul and Virginie, whom Felicity adores, go away to school; her nephew Victor, on whom she has lavished great affection, goes to sea as a cabin-boy and dies; Virginie contracts consumption and also dies. Felicity turns her attentions to refugees, to the chronic sick, and eventually to a parrot, Loulou, first alive, later stuffed. When the natural course of events has torn from her everybody to whom she has ever become emotionally attached—Paul being married and Mme Aubain dead—the process of deprivation and isolation is not complete. For already Felicity has begun to experience that deprivation of the senses not unusual in old age, firstly a growing deafness, later blindness. At the same time she has retained a naïve religious faith, in which her one remaining possession, the stuffed parrot, has become inextricably confused with the image of the Holy Ghost. The whole tale thus moves relentlessly through the process of denying Felicity all lasting and meaningful contact with the world outside herself—though 'meaningful' is a relative term, for the people involved, Theodore, the children, Victor and Mme Aubain, have only exploited her for their own profit. At the climax of the action, Felicity dedicates her one remaining possession, Loulou, to the religion with which she identifies him, by sending him to be carried in the procession for the Fête-Dieu. The famous final tableau, which has to be described to her by a neighbour, is really only accessible to her through her one remaining intact sense, smell: 'A blue vapour climbed up into Felicity's room. She strained her nostrils forward, drawing it in with a mystical sensuality.' As she dies, the apotheosis of the parrot Holy Spirit welcomes her to the supreme happiness. Dispossession of the things of this world has been identified with the attainment of the ultimate spiritual experience: '. . . and as she breathed her last breath, she thought she saw in the heavens opening above her a gigantic parrot soaring above her head'.

This process of gradual isolation is speeded up in the case of St Julian. Flaubert sticks fairly closely to the traditional form of the legend. The young Julian, who is an ardent huntsman, flees his family to avoid a prophecy that he will kill his own parents. He becomes rich and famous in exile, marries, but fulfils the prophecy by a terrible error. His crime is eventually expiated by service as hermit and ferryman, and he is received into heaven. In Flaubert's telling of the tale, the worldly and spiritual aspects of Julian's character are polarised from the start in his father's vision that the child will become a general and his mother's that he will become a saint. But he is soon torn from his family by the threat posed in the prophecy, and the attempt to achieve an alternative physical happiness is brought to an end by the frenzied murder of the old people who turn out to be his parents. As a hermit, Julian lives in the total seclusion from reality which the narrow walls of his hut aptly symbolise. His ascension to heaven is the natural climax to the process of purification.

In 'Herodias' the case is more complex, for the figure parallel to Felicity and Julian is already completely isolated from physical ties throughout the story; this is Iaokanann—John the Baptist— who is incarcerated in the deepest dungeon of Herod's palace at Machaerus. Apart from Samuel Beckett, no one has yet succeeded in making so complete a case of claustration the subject of a work of art. Flaubert uses John as an ever-present force rather than a central character, contrasting him with Herod, who is also a study in claustration but the complete antithesis to John. For Herod suffers from all the earthly bonds. He is politically confined in his citadel, though he burns within for power and conquests, as is symbolised by the pent-up vigour of the white stallions stabled deep inside the citadel. Equally, he is subject to the tyranny of the flesh, in the person of Salome; his lust for her overrides his religious scruples and leads him to sacrifice John. This contrast between John the ascetic and Herod the indulger is portrayed against a series of set-pieces recording the tensions and frustrations of politics, and the domination of gluttony and sexual greed over finer instinct, in a wide range of Roman and Jewish characters. Only John, by his death, achieves the happiness that others seek in material ends.

Or does he? Here is the nub of the problem. If in each of his tales Flaubert presents a figure who attains sainthood via a retreat into the self, it is not without carefully established ambiguity as to the value of the religious experience achieved. From the start of 'A Simple Heart' Felicity is shown as naïve, not to say stupid. If her desire to be shown on the map the whereabouts of Victor's house in Havana is used to satirise the nasty lawyer who makes fun of the innocent peasant, it is also a reminder of the limits of her intelligence. So that it is no surprise if her acceptance of religious doctrine and practice is unthinking. The confusion between parrot and cheap coloured postcards of the Holy Ghost leads to the delusion of the final image, the gigantic parrot hovering in heaven. And the tentative 'she thought she saw' stresses the individual, unvouchsafed nature of the vision.

In the case of St Julian, a similar undermining of the metaphysical element in the story is even more thoroughly carried out by the possible psychological interpretations left open by Flaubert. Julian's father has his vision of the child's future after a very heavy party; Julian's mother has hers in the exhausted state following childbirth. Julian's first act of destruction, the killing of a mouse in church, shows the child to have a straightforward sadistic streak. Is Julian perhaps something of an hysteric? Are the stag's prophecy, the mystic hunt before his parents' death and the final encounter with Christ not attributable to physical conditions and psychological malaise? Again, as with 'A Simple Heart', the final image is almost comic. Julian soars up to heaven in the arms of a Christ who has swelled until he bursts through the roof of the hermit's hut. The apotheosis is, to say the least, dubiously acceptable:

> Then the leper clasped him; and suddenly his eyes took on the brightness of the stars; his hair grew as long as the rays of the sun; the breath from his nostrils was as sweet as the scent of roses; a cloud of incense rose up from the room, the waters were singing. Yet an abundance of exquisite pleasure flooded down upon the soul of the swooning Julian; and he in whose arms he was so tightly held grew even bigger until his head and his feet touched the two walls of the hut. The roof flew off, the firmament unrolled; and Julian rose up towards the blue void, face to face with Our Lord Jesus Christ, who was carrying him up into heaven.

It is in 'Herodias' that the universal validity of individual religious experience is most thoroughly questioned. The climax to the story, John's decapitation, is the pendant to the portrait of a banquet which, not unlike a scene in Voltaire's *Zadig*, reduces all religious and philosophical beliefs to the same level by representing their adherents as similarly superstitious and intolerant. Flaubert takes care that the group of banqueters includes one Christian, for whom Iaokanann is the reincarnation of the prophet Elijah. The single-mindedness of John the Baptist and the sincerity of his self-sacrifice are not called into doubt. The truth of his revelation is quietly put into the perspective of other such beliefs and claims. This scene prepares us, in some measure, for the end of the tale. The apotheosis of John apparently concludes the story on a triumphant note. Had the last words been these, there would have been no doubt of the positive value of the message:

> One of the men said to him: 'Console yourself! He has descended among the dead to announce the coming of Christ.' Now the Essenian understood those words: 'I must diminish, that he may grow.'
> And all three of them, taking the head of Iaokanann, set off in the direction of Galilee.

But there is one more sentence, completely deflating the solemnity of the occasion:'As it was very heavy, they carried it alternately.' By this grotesque touch, the apotheosis, like that of Julian and Felicity, is reduced once more to an experience valid only for the individual himself.

Flaubert, in the *Trois contes*, suggests that, only within the self, purified of contact with the pressures and the attractions of the external world, is happiness and fulfilment possible, but that the religious experience which is the focus for such self-claustration is an entirely illusory one. If we compare the achievements of Felicity, Julian and John with those, in the novels, of Emma Bovary, Frédéric Moreau or St Antony, it is clear that the view of the self propounded in the *Trois contes* is consistent with that of the other works. Emma tries to translate her dissatisfaction with things as they are into a series of conventional images of happiness, and then to impose these images upon the people around her. Frédéric, his friend Deslauriers, and the whole generation for whom they are symbols, also try to match the yearnings of the inner self to the requirements of the external world. Such attempts are doomed to failure. Only St Antony learns the deceptiveness of the material world and the senses through which he has contact with it. He struggles through to the final victory, the vision of Christ:

> At last dawn came; and as when one lifts back the curtains of a tabernacle, golden clouds curling back in broad spirals uncovered the sky.
> In the very middle, in the disc of the sun itself, shone the face of Jesus Christ.

For the attentive reader this final vision is merely the ultimate delusion. To Flaubert the only meaningful world is indeed the inner world of the self, but its fulfilment can only be at the price of transcendent self-deception.

Self as perspective

As important to the development of prose fiction as the invasion of the self into the subject matter of stories and novels was the effect of the techniques of fiction introduced in order to express the limitations of individually perceived reality. The first modern novel, in this sense, is probably Benjamin Constant's *Adolphe* (1816). The eighteenth century had never questioned the assumption that character patterns are predictable and closely related to the social milieu in which a character evolves. A man develops linearly, affected only by new external influences. The realities of the world about him are capable of accurate analysis and record by the perceptive individual. When, in early nineteenth-century fiction, such as Chateaubriand's *René* (1805), a character is introduced who retrospectively reviews the actions and emotions of his own youth, there is no suggestion of a discontinuity between the past and present character of the narrator, nor is there any hint that the world about him can be seen differently from the way he sees it (cf Thackeray's *Henry Esmond*). *Adolphe*, however, despite its early date, poses exactly those problems. The younger Adolphe has lived through the traumatic experience of deliberately seducing Ellénore, another man's mistress, only to find himself in the classic ambiguous situation of being unable to live with her or without her. Within the narration itself the apparently sincere emotions leading to changes of heart during the course of the affair have been structured by the retrospective older Adolphe to form a narrative that exculpates himself by suggesting a tragedy, in which external forces, notably those of society, conspire to undermine the true emotional bond between himself and Ellénore. Where does the truth lie? What we know of Ellénore, of Adolphe's father and his father's friend the Baron de T . . . is, with the exception of isolated letters, filtered through the hero's own consciousness. So that our knowledge of the facts is contingent upon the gloss put upon them not only by the Adolphe who as actor of the original 'drama' experiences them but also by the Adolphe who as narrator reinterprets them. In a novel such as Jane Austen's *Emma* the distortion of facts by the protagonist is corrected for the reader by the author, but in *Adolphe* essential objective information is never available, for Constant resorts to stylistic ambiguities whenever he might be forced to take up a definite position. At the moment when Ellénore has yielded to the young Adolphe, the older Adolphe observes:

> Cursed be the man who in the first moments of a love relationship does not believe that this relationship must last forever! Cursed be the man who, in the arms of the mistress whom he has just won, retains a sense of doom, and foresees that the day will come when he will separate from her!

Is this a contrast with his own situation or a denunciation of himself? For clearly what he most appreciates in his newfound triumph is not the intrinsic value of the relationship but the status it gives him in the eyes of other men. What the reader derives from such ambiguities is an awareness of the inability of the individual to have a coherent view of his own conduct or an unbiased view of his environment. Even in retrospective analysis the temptation to erect falsely coherent structures in order to exculpate oneself becomes overwhelming.

If everything that Adolphe sees and feels is coloured by his own personality, how much more true is this of the characters of Flaubert's novels. Constant suggests that the external world exerts harmful pressures upon the inner man. Flaubert suggests that it offers dangerous distractions. For Emma Bovary and Frédéric Moreau see the world as their moods dictate, reality becoming thereby a strictly relative concept. Our appreciation of *Madame Bovary* as a novel depends upon our awareness of the multiplicity of points of view so orchestrated that no one character has a truer vision of the world than any other. In the novels of Stendhal or Balzac, as in most nineteenth-century English novels, the surface of society is carefully conveyed to us by the author, however critical he may be of that surface. The world therefore is a unity. For Flaubert there are no such truths, only questions of perspective. *Madame Bovary* explores not merely the disastrous gap between Emma's view of reality and an actual reality, but the gap between the conspiracy of society to call certain things reality and the attempt of Emma herself, hampered by the limitations of conventional language, to penetrate beyond the world of agreed conventions to inner truths valid perhaps only for herself. Somewhat of a blend of Dorothea and Rosamund in George Eliot's *Middlemarch*, Emma dimly perceives the possibility of a higher communion of souls; but to achieve it she wrongly attempts to mould each man she meets—dull but loyal Charles, philandering Rodolphe, weak and pretentious Léon—to her own ideal image. By a revolutionary technique Flaubert allows us to see this process of miscomprehension as it takes place, for we view the world for a substantial part of the central portion of the novel from Emma's own viewpoint. This technique is equally important in *Education sentimentale*. There it often matters little what a person or event really is, but merely how Frédéric perceives them. Mme Arnoux, his ideal woman, might seem to us a dull, virtuous and not particularly intelligent middle-class housewife; that is certainly how she seems to one of the other characters in the novel—though not one whose opinions we should care to share. But for Frédéric the aura that surrounds her on his first sight of her is never dispelled:

> She was like the women in Romantic novels. He would not have wished to add or subtract a single detail in her person. The universe had just, on a sudden, grown broader. She was the point of light on which the totality of things was converging.

Frédéric's whole progress through life is governed by such visions. But whereas in his moments of frustration or disillusion the prostitute Rosanette may seem trivial or the banker's wife Mme Dambreuse may look like a crystallised apricot, Mme Arnoux, whom he barely attempts to possess on a physical level, retains almost to the last that same luminosity of his first vision.

In confining the reader within the perspective of one or more characters, what Constant and Flaubert have in common, despite differences of subject matter and style, is the emphasis they give to the distorting power of language. For language is the entity which, by appearing to identify common elements in all men's experience, disguises the unique nature of individual perceptions. Writing on religion Constant said:

> All our inmost feelings seem to elude the grasp of language. The rebellious world, by the very fact of generalising what it expresses, serves to designate and to distinguish, rather than to define. As an instrument of the mind it is only good at conveying the notions of the mind. It fails in anything which has to do with the senses, on the one hand, or the soul, on the other.

His views accord closely with the key passage in *Madame Bovary* where the reader is warned against accepting too readily that hostile judgement of Emma that her own woman's-magazine silliness seems to justify. Emma, in her rendezvous with Rodolphe, has been becoming more and more reliant on the sentimental cliché to convey the strength of her emotions, to the point where the conventional protestations of affection seem to her sated lover merely tiresome:

> Emma was like all mistresses; and the charm of novelty, dropping gradually away like a garment, revealed the eternal monotony of passion, which always takes the same forms and uses the same language.

At which point, Flaubert, in a rare example of authorial intervention, steps in not only to criticise Rodolphe, whose thoughts he has just transcribed, but also to defend explicitly his own point of view:

> So full of experience as he was, he could not distinguish the difference in the emotions beneath the similarity of the expression; as if the fullness of the soul did not sometimes brim over in the emptiest of metaphors, since no one, ever, can give the exact measure of his needs nor his ideas, nor his sorrows, and human speech is like a cracked cauldron on which one beats out tunes for the bears to dance to, when one is trying to bring tears to the eyes of the stars.

Thus Constant and Flaubert both hit upon that corrupting power of language which purports to communicate while preventing meaningful communication. The viewpoint of the individual is the only valid psychological standpoint from which to examine a fictional world; but that individual's whole interpretation of the world must itself be regarded with suspicion, as it is subject to deformation by the very words in which it is couched. For a novelist this is an extreme position at which to arrive. (It was to be explored further by Marcel Proust, Virginia Woolf and their heirs, in the following century.) For poets it was a view readily shared by many of Flaubert's contemporaries. It is to the great poets of the period that one must look for the fullest attempt to re-order the world according to the perceptions of the self, and for the widest exploration of new collocations of linguistic elements designed to distort as little as possible the substance of these perceptions.

THE SELF AS VISIONARY

As early as Rousseau's *Rêveries d'un promeneur solitaire*, we find a writer describing a state of mind in which the sensation of the outside world is merely the minimum necessary to stimulate awareness of his own existence, and where the creations of his own mind acquire an equivalent reality with the world of nature. The pleasures of this passive state were to be fully enlarged upon by Lamartine and Musset. But its significance, the alternative reality which it seemed to suggest, was rather obscured. Nineteenth-century poets often saw themselves as visionaries, but for poets like Hugo, Vigny and Leconte de Lisle the special perceptions that the poet possessed were derived from, and used to explain, a reality external to him. The first major artist of the period to question whether the inner experience of man, especially states of dream and daydream, were not equally important ways of access to universal truths was Gérard de Nerval (1808–55).

Nerval

In his prose work *Les Filles du feu* (1854) there is a key antithesis between men of action and dreamers, in which the latter are the more sympathetic though also the more unhappy. Of the rather disparate pieces that form the collection, the story 'Sylvie' best illustrates the importance to the writer's self of the experiences offered by the dream state. The narrator, in love with the image of a woman as projected across the footlights by a certain actress, realises as he muses drowsily over events from his childhood that the actress resembles the object of a similarly impossible childhood love, Adrienne, a girl who became a nun. Shunning these ideal figures, he takes a journey into his own past to see another former love, Sylvie, in the hope that she by her reality will exorcise the fascination of his dream-woman. He attempts to poeticise Sylvie into a substitute for Adrienne, but comes to realise that the two elements—the ideal, of which actress and nun are the image, and the real, the flesh-and-blood Sylvie— are incompatible. Since the essence of an ideal is that it can never be possessed, the object of his love is at its most real when embodied in the dream's re-experience of the past rather than when transferred into the substitute of the physical present.

In *Aurelia* (1855) Nerval expands upon this idea. A substantial part of this openly autobiographical work portrays states of dream and hallucination, but he defends his right to explore what might seem exclusively personal material:

> If I did not think that a writer's mission is to analyse sincerely what he experiences in the grave circumstances of life, and if I did not set myself a task which I consider useful, I would stop now, and would not attempt to describe what I subsequently experienced in a series of visions that were perhaps mad, or, by average standards, sick . . .

What Nerval—like Coleridge and his circle—sees in these non-rational experiences is 'a new life . . . liberated from the conditions of time and space, and similar perhaps to the life that awaits us after death'. In dreams the self continues the work of existence but in another form, so that by considering the world of dreams (and Nerval therewith includes daydreams and the intermediate states of consciousness) one can draw valid conclusions about human nature as a whole. Nerval is not, then, denying the validity of material reality and rational perception but proposing the complementary value of the two states. Though the narrative of *Aurelia* is chronological, the events that compose it have no rational linearity and cannot usefully be summarised. What Nerval derives from his inner exploration is nothing less than an account of spiritual salvation.

The same is true of the sonnet sequence, *Les Chimères*, his major achievement as a writer. Here the logical discontinuity between sonnets is less disorientating for the reader than the transitions of *Aurelia*. *Les Chimères* offers us Nerval's perceptions of the nature of the universe, of the relation of man to the universe, and of the forces within man himself, as these issues impinge on his inner persona. The five sonnets of 'Christ in the Olive Grove' express the tensions deriving from the possibility that the universe is a chaos uninformed by the creative presence of God—Christian or otherwise— a doubt raised in a different set of images in 'Delfica'. In each case, though the presence of a divinity is affirmed, its benevolence is left unestablished. At the same time 'Golden Verses' places man in the perspective of the rest of creation, rejecting the rationalist and sceptical accounts of the universe in favour of one where man is an equal partner only if he recognises the powers inherent in what surrounds him.

The rest of the sonnets portray the struggle for the perfection which can only be achieved by the harmonising of the self into the universal continuum, the suppression of the ego in perfect love. In each case—'Artemis', 'Horus', 'Anteros'—the poem records a failure, for the male principle is attacked or denied, and without the male principle the universe is barren and hence destined to destruction. Only in 'Myrtho' and 'El Desdichado' is there a sense of achievement; in the second case, significantly, through the transcendent power of art. 'El Desdichado' is a key to the structure of the other poems in that it shows how the tensions within Nerval—symbolised by antitheses such as the opposition between the rationality and light of Mediterranean classicism and the emotivity and gloom of northern gothicism— can be synthesised in the figure and function of the artist himself. This is in no sense a solution to the philosophical dilemma, but it provides a justification for the expression in personal images of a problem which Nerval naturally felt to be common to all men. So we may define the creative function of the self for Nerval as the formulation of that series of dream images—Pausilippus, dying gods, volcanoes—which emotionally conveys a metaphysical experience not capable of analysis or communication in logical terms. 'I thought I understood that there was a bond between the external and the internal world; that only inattention or mental disorder distorted the obvious relationship', he wrote in *Aurelia*. *Les Chimères* and the short stories are the guidebook to his voyages between the two worlds.

Baudelaire

Almost contemporaneously with Nerval, Charles Baudelaire (1821–67) was similarly exploring the possibility that the intuitive perceptions of the poet can isolate truths not accessible to the rational, analytical mind. It was also his belief, as he expressed it in the autobiographical *My Heart Laid Bare*, that 'When every individual sets his heart on spiritual advancement, then, and only then, will humanity be on the road to progress'. The combination of these beliefs is to be found throughout Baudelaire's work, both in the critical essays collected as *Aesthetic Curiosities* and *Romantic Art* and in his collections of poetry *Les Fleurs du Mal* and *Spleen de Paris* (the prose poems). For him, it is the task of the artist to throw light on man's spiritual problems by looking at the material world in a new way. He is very insistent on the importance of examining the modern world as it is, warts and all, with no retreat into a pre-conceived range of 'beautiful' subjects. In practice this leads to a poetry which is metaphysical in implication but highly concrete in subject. This is not as paradoxical as it sounds for, though Baudelaire, like Balzac, Gautier and Nerval, was influenced by the Swedish mystic Swedenborg into seeing material objects as manifestations of abstract values, he also felt that there existed more immediately perceivable horizontal correspondences between objects, so that the first step towards a comprehension of the abstract should be to re-order one's concepts of the concrete. The classic exposition of this idea is in his poem 'Correspondances':

> *La Nature est un temple où de vivants piliers*
> *Laissent parfois sortir de confuses paroles;*

L'homme y passe à travers des forêts de symboles
Qui l'observent avec des regards familiers.

Comme de longs échos qui de loin se confondent
Dans une ténébreuse et profonde unité,
Vaste comme la nuit et comme la clarté,
Les parfums, les couleurs et les sons se répondent.

Il est des parfums frais comme des chairs d'enfants,
Doux comme les hautbois, verts comme les prairies,
Et d'autres, corrompus, riches et triomphants,

Ayant l'expansion des choses infinies,
Comme l'ambre, le musc, le benjoin et l'encens,
Qui chantent les transports de l'esprit et des sens.

[Nature is a temple where living pillars sometimes let forth confused words; in it man goes through forests of symbols which watch him with familiar looks.

Like long echoes which from a distance mingle into a shadowy and deep unity, as vast as night and light, perfumes, colours and sounds reply to one another.

There are perfumes fresh as children's flesh, sweet as oboes, green as meadows, and others corrupt, rich and triumphant,

Sharing the capacity of expansion that infinite things have, such as amber, musk, balsam and incense, which hymn the transports of the mind and the senses.]

What this poem suggests is not a specific mystical message, but the way an alert mind and the imaginative interpretation of acute sense experiences should at least awaken in man the awareness of the infinite dimensions behind conventional surfaces.

The absence of a categorical interpretation of nature in this poem is not an individual instance of failure. For the whole of *Les Fleurs du Mal*—and the prose poems can be regarded as intensifying aspects of that collection rather than extending its range in any significant way—is the record of an exploration of life which seems guaranteed to stop short of the revelation it is seeking. For Baudelaire, man is only really alive when he is aware, and the enemy of awareness is convention. The result of this is that the poet, in his determination to retain awareness, is driven constantly on to new experiences, because as he grows accustomed to the old ones they lose their power to stimulate his imaginative perceptions. It is the image of the voyage that shapes the collection, and the attendant images of the sea, ships, clouds, exotic worlds ever beyond the horizon; while, in antithesis to the eternal voyage, there is the theme of stasis as embodied in the stupefying experience of *ennui*, the state in which no element of conventional reality seems capable of awakening in the poet the sense that he even exists, a state of living nullity.

The dilemma in which the poet finds himself is that, though his metaphysical goal is God, good, beauty—the precise identity and inter-relationship of the three being hotly disputed by critics—the experiences needed to sharpen his sense of existence lead him farther and farther down into ugliness, evil and Satan. In the poems of the section 'Spleen and Ideal', he seeks for meaning in love but is forced to move from sensual indulgence to spiritual attachment and finally into a masochistic relationship in which passion and suffering are inseparable. In each case the woman is no more than a vehicle for the poet's attempt to break through to some ultimate experience. In many poems a single feature, physical or psychological, transports the poet beyond immediate physical reality. In 'Exotic Perfume' it is 'the scent of your warm breasts' that conjures up images of tropical paradise; in 'The Hair' the woman's rich black hair becomes the infinite waves of the sea, the deep blue of the sky, 'a whole distant world, absent, almost dead'. In 'The Living Torch' the eyes are seen as the candles of a sacred mass; in 'Lowering Sky' they introduce the mists and cold of a winter landscape. Yet at the end no aspect of love is sufficient to sustain in the poet 'the art of evoking the happy moments', and he relapses into the dreaded *ennui*.

Pluviose, irrité contre la ville entière,
De son urne à grands flots verse un froid ténébreux
Aux pâles habitants du voisin cimetière
Et la mortalité sur les faubourgs brumeux.

Mon chat sur le carreau cherchant une litière
Agite sans repos son corps maigre et galeux;
L'âme d'un vieux poëte erre dans la gouttière
Avec la triste voix d'un fantôme frileux.

Le bourdon se lamente, et la bûche enfumée
Accompagne en fausset la pendule enrhumée,
Cependant qu'en un jeu plein de sales parfums,

Heritage fatal d'une vieille hydropique,
Le beau valet de coeur et la dame de pique
Causent sinistrement de leurs amours défunts.

[February, in his anger against the whole city, pours a shadowy cold gushing forth from his urn upon the pale inhabitants of the neighbouring cemetery, and mortality upon the foggy suburbs.

My cat, looking for a place to rest on the tiles, ceaselessly moves his thin, mangy body; the soul of an old poet is straying in the gutter with the sad voice of a chill phantom.

The bell bewails its lot, and the smoking log accompanies the wheezing clock in falsetto, while in a pack of cards full of filthy smells,

Fatal legacy of a dropsical old woman, the handsome knave of hearts and the queen of spades talk in sinister fashion of their departed loves.]

The poet's humanity has drained out into the objects around him. His restlessness has been absorbed by the cat, his depressed physical and mental condition by the bell, the log, the clock. Most sinister of all, his very past, his love-life, has been taken over by the pack of cards. As if this living death were not frightening enough, 'The Clock', the poem that closes 'Spleen and Ideal', reminds us that while man, in his state of *ennui*, has the illusion of standing still, time does not. In images that pile up into a relentless speeding crescendo, Baudelaire suggests the destructive power of time as arrow, time as mosquito sucking man's life blood, time as the card-player who never loses. Only in the intense pleasure of new experience is time suspended, as it were. Since the power of love to create that suspension has been drained away, the poet must move on to something else.

In the next section, 'Pictures of Paris', Baudelaire investigates the inspirational possibilities of the objective world around him, starting from the physical facts of ugliness and poverty, and working towards a spiritual landscape of urban man. Here we sense, perhaps for the first time, the degree to which the poet fears satiety above all else, when in the poem 'Gaming' he portrays the need for a passion, however ugly and pointless. Though the clientèle of the gaming salon have lost their human quality in any conventional sense—'faces without lips, lips without colour, jaws without teeth'—and are reduced to objects, as the click of metal and stone in the prostitutes' ear-rings symbolises, they retain meaning by the very existence of their fanaticism for gambling; whereas the poet sees himself as the detached observer:

> *Et mon coeur s'effraya d'envier maint pauvre homme*
> *Courant avec ferveur à l'abîme béant,*
> *Et qui, soûl de son sang, préférerait en somme*
> *La douleur à la mort et l'enfer au néant!*

[And my heart scared itself by envying many a poor man running ardently to the gaping abyss, and who, drunk on his own blood, in short would prefer pain to death and hell to nothingness!]

From the outer world Baudelaire progresses with increasing frenzy through the stimulation of drugs and intoxicants ('Wine'), and perversion ('Flowers of Evil') to the logical extreme of revolt, satanism ('Revolt'). But the climax of the collection is its final section, 'Death'. For death represents the ultimate new experience and, as such, it offers the same fascinations and fears as the sources of inspiration already explored. The first poem of the section, 'The Death of the Lovers', presents an ecstatic vision of brilliant light and the one-ness of twin hearts that has much in common with the union of Malivert and Spirite at the end of Gautier's story. The emphasis of the poem in the final tercet is on the power of death to give new validity to a faded experience:

> *Et plus tard un Ange, entr'ouvrant les portes,*
> *Viendra ranimer, fidèle et joyeux,*
> *Les miroirs ternis et les flammes mortes.*

[And later an angel, half-opening the doors, will come faithfully and joyously to bring back life to the tarnished mirrors and the dead flames.]

Eventually, however, the obsessive idea returns that even in death the power of habit may impose the return of *ennui*. In 'The Dream of an Inquisitive Person' this fear is powerfully transposed into the nightmare of the poet as spectator watching the curtain go up on what proves to be merely the familiar experience:

> *J'étais mort sans surprise, et la terrible aurore*
> *M'enveloppait—Eh quoi! n'est-ce donc que cela?*
> *La toile était levée et j'attendais encore*

[I had died without surprise, and the terrible dawn enveloped me— What? Is this all it is? The curtain was up, and I was still waiting.]

However, the vision is only a nightmare, and not, as with the other experiences exhausted during the course of the collection, an attested reality. The final long poem, 'The Voyage', which is almost an index to the principal ideas and images of the rest of *Fleurs du Mal*, reiterates that the essential is the search itself. 'The true travellers are only those who set out for the sake of setting out'. In the attempt to retain awareness, the essential for any man hoping to penetrate beyond the conventional view of reality, the traveller must abandon accepted standards of morality and aesthetics. For everything contains its opposite; there is no God without Satan, nor beauty without ugliness. And underlying both this poem and the whole collection is the tacit admission that by definition the seeker cannot attain his goal, for attainment is stasis and *ennui*. Hence the acceptance of death as the extension of the voyage rather than its terminus:

> *O Mort, vieux capitaine, il est temps! levons l'ancre!*
> *Ce pays nous ennuie, ô Mort! Appareillons!*
> *Si le ciel et la mer sont noirs comme de l'encre,*
> *Nos coeurs que tu connais sont remplis de rayons!*
>
> *Verse-nous ton poison pour qu'il nous réconforte!*
> *Nous voulons, tant ce feu nous brûle le cerveau,*
> *Plonger au fond du gouffre, Enfer ou Ciel, qu'importe?*
> *Au fond de l'inconnu pour trouver du nouveau!*

[Oh Death, old captain, it is time, let us weigh anchor. This land bores us, oh Death, let us get under way, If the sky and the sea are black as ink, our hearts which you know are full of light.

Pour us your poison to strengthen us. This fire so burns our brains that we want to plunge into the bottom of the gulf, Hell or Heaven, what does it matter? To the depths of the unknown in search of the new!]

Baudelaire's greatest contribution to the tradition of the visionary self was probably the breaking down of the traditional categories of sense perception and the greater freedom of imaginative expression which his resultant theory and practice of *correspondances* achieved. But in terms of verse form and diction he is quite conservative, falling easily into the habits of Romantic rhetoric still fashionable among contemporaries, such as Hugo. It was for his successors, notably Tristan Corbière and Jules Laforgue, to extend the poetic means by which the visionary could transmit his visions.

Corbière

For Corbière, vision implies no metaphysical dimension. His task is to analyse himself as a representative of man's condition in a nihilistic epoch. His poetry is almost exclusively confined to the single slim volume, *Amours jaunes* (1873), a collection which, like

Fleurs du Mal, has a roughly definable structure. It is divided into six sections: 'Yellow Loves', 'Serenade of Serenades', 'Flukes', 'Armorica', 'Seamen' and 'Rondels for Afterwards'. The first three of these revolve around the separate or combined themes of the city and of woman, but under these headings are a number of sub-themes: the ideal of love and its disillusion ('Steamboat', 'Noble Lady'); relations between the sexes as a violent perpetual struggle ('To the Eternal Woman', 'Feminine Singular'); the affectation of freedom and other poses of man in the face of an indifferent society ('Chic Bohemian'); the obsession with physical ugliness, particularly the poet's own ('Good Fortune and Fortune', 'The Toad'). Poetry itself is a sub-theme too, for the city and woman are seen as necessary sources of inspiration, and in 'The Contumacious Poet', the final poem of the first section, literature is portrayed as cutting the poet off from the possibility of establishing human contact in a natural surrounding. The ultimate experience conveyed here is that of disgust, disillusion, isolation. In the city the stress is on the sordid and false. The sordidness is seen in terms of poverty, ugliness and prostitution; the pathetic human comedy of pimps, whores, drunks and beggars, with the 'I' figure of the poems constantly debased in his own estimation to a state lower even than the world around him—the falseness is conveyed by theatrical metaphors and pictures of nature reduced to artifice. As for woman, she is either idealised and unobtainable or cynically mocked as an enemy, in poems of increasing sadism. In the most violent poems the central self is projected into a position of triumphant domination over women. But consistently the overall result is that of failure. For it is failure and isolation that characterise the poet, who is isolated from society through his obsession with literature, and from love by his physical deformity. This isolation finds its most complete expression in 'Pariah', the last poem of 'Flukes'. Using the Breton bird of ill-omen—'Me, I'm the lean cuckoo'—Corbière shows himself unable to conform to the domestic norms of human society, unable to possess woman, to hold a coherent ideal, to possess a determined direction in life, 'As for me my path lies behind me'.

To this point Corbière's poetry can be said to assume the triple function of the analysis, definition and communication of the causes of his spiritual distress, to show the unsuccessful attempt to escape from his own limitations into the mask of the dominator, the cynical gallant, the traditional hero—all masks soon revealed empty. The first truly visionary element, the touching upon sleep and dream as potential sources of new, possibly higher, experiences, is found in the 'Litany of Sleep' in 'Flukes'. The poet, in his invocation of sleep, runs over all the moral and physical ills of life, and sees sleep as providing a provisional death for these ills and a source of happiness for the sleeper. The edge of sleep is a visionary state, but sleep itself brings the full liberation of dream. Dream operates firstly by giving free rein to the subconscious, which is the gateway to the new world, Baudelaire's 'deeps of the unknown', a world outside the control of ordinary logic. In Corbière's own words it is a 'land where the dumb reveals himself a prophet'. The function of the vision communicated by the verse is the apprehension of a spiritual mystery: the power of the soul liberated from earthly clay, its communion with eternal forces, its ability to procure happiness for the wretched.

Sleep and dream are not, however, seen as conclusive escape from the degradation of urban reality and the isolation of the creative artist. Though the vision of the world of sleep dominates the centre of 'Litany of Sleep', it is the suggestion of insomnia and the condemnation of the *bon bourgeois* sleeping his dreamless sleep that form the framework to the poem. The real antidote, though not the solution, to the pessimism of the first three sections of the collection lies in sections four to six. Here the poet is concerned with Brittany and with the sea. Not that this is in any sense a lucky or optimistic world, as the first two poems of 'Armorica' show, with their stress on unhealthiness and ill-omen. But it is a world of calm, fatalistic reality, uncorrupted by the sham of the city. The acceptance of fate eliminates the mental turmoil of man obsessed with life's possibilities. Furthermore all that is esteemed in urban society is valueless here, and poverty and ugliness become tolerable, simply because they are respected. The sea and the sailors, connected with Brittany through the ports such as Roscoff, provide the final dimension of escape, for they are the example of group solidarity and independence within the framework of Breton practicality and fatalism. Corbière indulges in a Lawrentian romanticisation of simplicity and virility by a studied stress on rough realism. His sailors are a race apart, only corrupted by their contact with the land: men accustomed to hardship, violence, mute brotherhood in the face of danger; men in love with adventure and above all with the sea itself. Though the details of the sordidness of their life are unromanticised, the philosophy which underlies the portrait is essentially that of the poet presenting an ideal world into which he cannot penetrate. Corbière translates the paradise of Baudelaire's 'Anywhere out of this world' into a society where, as in Flaubert's 'A Simple Heart', happiness is available at the price of an insensitivity which the poet, by the mere fact of being a poet, is denied.

Corbière's importance lies, however, less in the solipsistic nature of his world view (after all, even Baudelaire's claim to have perceptions relevant to all men is a highly dubious one) than in his development of a poetic medium that, by fracturing conventions of imagery, syntax and lexical register, attempts to overcome that distorting force of language against which the characters of Flaubert struggle in vain. In Corbière's vocabulary, technical terms, archaisms, neologisms and foreign expressions jostle with literary formulae and slang. By switching rapidly through a series of different verbal levels the poet can establish a high degree of register incoherence. Take, for example, this stanza from '*Veder Napoli poi mori*', part of the satirical picture of Italian customs officials which forms the basic image for the denigration of the traditional nineteenth-century picture of Italian spiritual values.

> *O Corinne!—ils sont là déclamant sur ma malle . . .*
> *Lasciate speranza, mes cigares dedans!*
> *O Mignon . . . ils ont tout éclos mon linge sale*
> *Pour le passer au bleu de l'éternel printemps.*

[Oh Corinne!—they are there declaiming over my trunk . . .
Abandon all hope, my cigars inside! Oh my sweet! . . . They have
all ope'd my dirty washing to bleach it in the blue of eternal
spring.]

Here there are three literary references: 'Corinne', which conjures up the image of Italy portrayed in Mme de Staël's *Corinne,
or Italy*; 'Abandon all hope', quoted from Dante; and the image in
'Mignon' and '*éclos*' based on a famous poem by the sixteenth-
century poet, Ronsard—*Mignonne, allons voir si la rose/Qui ce
matin avoit déclose/Sa robe de pourpre au soleil.* But 'ope'd' is used in
the new context not of Ronsard's rosebud but of Corbière's dirty
washing; the mock poetic diction of '*au bleu de l'éternel printemps*'
is undermined by the fact that '*passer au bleu*' is normal spoken
diction for 'to bleach' of linen; the grandeur of the Dante reference
is deflated by the prosaic cigars, and so on. Throughout the choice
of words, structure and images, this principle of disjunction,
paradox and sardonic association of the normally unrelated is
used to awaken the reader to a new vision of all levels of reality
—an aspect of the poet's work that was to attract such poets as
T. S. Eliot. If Corbière has little to say about metaphysical vision,
he frequently succeeds in re-ordering one's perceptions of life.

Laforgue

Jules Laforgue combines the philosophical obsessions of
Baudelaire with the technical virtuosity of Corbière. His thought
is dominated by the need for an explanation of life that would
restore a sense of the eternal without contradicting the deterministic and rationalistic view of the observable world. This need
he couples with a sense of the pointlessness of material reality, of
the insignificance of man within the scale of the universe, and of a

sense of evil implicit in the very condition of being. His source for many of these ideas was German Romantic philosophy; for, if Baudelaire and his contemporaries were nurtured on Swedenborg, it was to Schopenhauer that the generation of the 1870s turned. Laforgue was particularly interested in the downgrading of material phenomena involved in such philosophy. The world was held to exist meaningfully only in the sense that a given eye so perceives it. The individual's perceptions then form the basis for a structure of temporal, spatial and causal relationships, but no ultimate meaning can be attributed to such a structure, for it remains relative to the individual perceiver. Ultimate meaning has to lie in non-physical eternal forces, in the case of Schopenhauer's theories in the will, which invests all things. Since the senses offer no reliable evidence of eternal forces, the way to an understanding of this will can only be by exploration inward, into the human psyche. Through the process of self-mortification, both spiritual and physical (eg, chastity) certain people can attain a contemplative vision of the truth as embodied in this all-pervasive force of will. To his reading of Schopenhauer, Laforgue added the ideas of Hartmann on the unconscious—not the psychological entity of the Freudians but a pantheistic principle serving to reconcile idealism and determinism. Via Hartmann, Laforgue accepts a pessimistic view of progress whereby man will evolve nihilistically towards a rejection of material existence, and will finally, by a sort of suicide of the species, prefer unity with the unconscious through death to the inherent evil of life.

This philosophical position had important consequences for Laforgue's aesthetic beliefs. Since the individual perceives the material world and his dreams equally vividly, each is equally valid. Given that the unconscious is present in every individual and is in a state of constant evolution, then art, which aspires continuously to express the unconscious (the artist being especially gifted for communication with, and expression of, this mystic world-spirit, for reasons that Laforgue does not make clear), must evolve too, rejecting all form of convention in rules, clichés and traditional patterns. The artist will take his own ephemeral perceptions and, through the lightning intuition of identities and relationships, will reveal aspects of eternal truths. There are, of course, substantial problems in this view of art. If the artist's perceptions of the unconscious are all through aesthetic intuitions, all creation will become an intuitional and involuntary act. But it is by definition impossible to give a verbal equivalent to pure intuition without distorting it. It is also impossible to assess the aesthetic validity of the expression since the only person able to judge whether the experience is betrayed by its expression is the artist who underwent the original perception. However, such an aesthetic has three practical effects. First, the idea of unconscious in a proto-surrealist sense allows the exploration of that inner part of the self which is to be in contact with the universal unconscious. Second, the need for constant renewal of form justifies experimentalism in the face of the formalism at that time being preached by critics such as Taine. Third, the admission of ephemeral experience permitted the acceptance of Baudelaire's views on the value of the urban and of transitory fashion as matter for poetry.

Laforgue's earliest verse was the collection *Le Sanglot de la Terre* (unpublished in his lifetime) on which he was working in about 1880. It betrays his philosophical preoccupations clearly, without more than hinting at his aesthetic attitudes, a factor which probably led to his decision not to publish it. The central theme of the poems is the pointlessness of existence, both human and inorganic, but with man's temporality in general, and the poet's in particular, as focus. This subdivides naturally into, on the one hand, expressions of the vanity of human life, the essential evil of mankind, the triviality of human action and emotion, and, on the other, the consideration of cosmic forces and the eternal principle underlying the universe. The link between the two sides is the sun symbol, a life principle yet itself subject to cosmic decay. When he moved on to the poems which were to form *Les Com-*

plaintes (1885) and *L' Imitation de Notre Dame La Lune* (1886), the perceptible change in his work was not of inspiration but of expression. As early as 1882 he had written of excluding statement from poetry: 'I dream of poetry which *says* nothing, but is snatches of dreaming not coherently ordered. The attempt to say something, to expound, to prove something, leads to prose.' Rather than use a direct poetic address to the reader, the Laforgue of *Complaintes*—like the Eliot of *The Waste Land*—fragments his 'self' into a multiple personality, speaking sometimes as one voice, sometimes two, sometimes as a chorus. The themes of the flight from life through death or symbolic death (exile, chastity or other forms of self-denial) and the attack upon the two great life forces—woman, who as fecundity is responsible for life's continuance, and *ennui*, the mood in which an excess of intelligence indulging in intense introspection makes the pain of existence most acute—are now explored through a host of frequently recurring images. *Ennui*, for example, is associated with bells, the wind, the colour grey, the sound of the barrel-organ and, above all, Sunday, Laforgue's 'ever-spleen day', when the absence of work, and the conventional rituals of religion emphasise the pointlessness of existence. The poet's position is complicated by the sense that, though the surest way to eradicate *ennui* is self-obliteration, he is not prepared for death. This tension is most clear in his treatment of woman. Though in her fecund aspect the ally of time and associate of sun, summer and warmth, she is also the soul complementary to the poet's, the '*Elle*' towards whom his vain, personal eternal search for pure love is directed, the moon, purity and sterility. As with Baudelaire, all experience takes on the paradoxical possession of its own opposite; as with Corbière, the expression of these tensions is made to involve fracturing of syntax, coupling of incompatible lexical registers, every type of thematic and verbal opposition that will enhance the sense of fundamental dualities.

L' *Imitation de Notre Dame la Lune* represents the highest point in Laforgue's coupling of philosophy with poetic experiment. The whole collection is centred on the interrelated images of moon and Pierrot, with the poet as subjective observer initially, when the character of the moon is being established, but passing into a projected voice within the character of Pierrot, noticeably in the 'Sayings of Pierrot' which make up half the cycle. Pierrot brings with him the traditions of Watteau's *Gilles*, the associations of the *commedia dell' arte* character and the Shakespearian 'wise fool'. The moon is a projection of Laforgue's own fantasy: 'I love . . . to imagine your climate, and flora and fauna for I know only the art of invention as a way of offering you my troubles.' Both symbols have common ground in the themes of sterility and purity, but each extends into quite separate fields, the religious and magic associations of the moon, the pose and mask of Pierrot. The poetry thus created has a curious tension between intellectualism and emotion. The intellect must be constantly in play to absorb the cultural allusions accruing round the Pierrot figure, but the language itself, with its constant metaphor throwing together entirely disparate elements and playing with assonance, rhyme and rhythm almost for their own sake, is not intellectually accessible. T. S. Eliot, in his essay 'The Metaphysical Poets' (1921), observed that during the process of composition a poet's mind is inert or neutral towards his experience (including his emotions and his reading alike), while the work of creation is being done by his sensibility. The corollary of this, which Eliot does not explore, is the interrelation of intellect and sensibility on the part of the reader. For, to comprehend *L'Imitation*, the reader has to 'feel' the poet's thought, to use Eliot's phrase, 'as immediately as the odour of a rose'.

But the Laforgue who was so profoundly to affect Pound and Eliot is not so much the poet of *Les Complaintes* or even *L'Imitation* as the poet of *Derniers vers*, posthumously published in 1890. As far back as 1881 Laforgue had written: 'I dream of a form of poetry which would be psychology in the shape of a dream, with flowers, wind, inextricable symphonies with a melodic phrase (a subject) whose pattern recurs from time to time.' Such an aim entailed the rejection of philosophy as a subject and of form as a conscious game. In their place is an orchestrated synthesis of images of the eternal natural cycle, in which the meaninglessness of life is an inherent quality, rather than an explicit attitude, and a new fluid poetic form from which the dangers of logical deformation are banished by the exclusion of all formal arrangements and the suppression of all parts of language, even conventional syntactic necessities, that do not add to emotional communication. The verse thus becomes a structure of associations and feelings expressive of deliberately unresolved complexities. Around the familiar themes that hold the collection together —the seasons, musical instruments, Sunday and other bourgeois rituals, the pariah, the various manifestations of woman—there accumulate complex networks of secondary images, physical and abstract, Thus in 'Winter Coming' there are a series of images of rain and damp, another series of references to wind and scudding clouds, and so on through the full range of autumnal associations, falling leaves, mists and sun that has no warmth.

> *On ne peut plus s'asseoir, tous les bancs sont mouillés;*
> *Crois-moi, c'est bien fini jusqu'à l'année prochaine,*
> *Tant les bancs sont mouillés, tant les bois sont rouillés,*
> *Et tant les cors ont fait ton ton, ont fait ton taine! . . .*
>
> *Ah! nuées accourues des côtes de la Manche,*
> *Vous nous avez gâté notre dernier dimanche!*
>
> *Il bruine;*
> *Dans la forêt mouillée, les toiles d'araignées*
> *Ploient sous les gouttes d'eau, et c'est leur ruine . . .*

[One can no longer sit down, all the benches are wet; believe me, it's all well and truly over till next year, the benches are so wet, the benches are so rusty, and the horns have so sounded tantivi, have sounded tantara.

Oh! clouds speeding here from the Channel coast, you've spoilt our last Sunday for us!

It's drizzling; in the damp forest, the spiders' webs bend beneath the drops of water, and it is their ruin . . .]

But the rural vocabulary is there only for the sense of season; the action is played out, like Eliot's 'Prufrock', against a drab urban, indeed suburban, décor.

> *Mais, lainages, caoutchoucs, pharmacie, rêve,*
> *Rideaux écartés du haut des balcons des grèves*
> *Devant l'océan de toitures des faubourgs,*
> *Lampes, estampes, thé, petits-fours,*
> *Serez-vous pas mes seules amours! . . .*
> *(Oh! et puis, est-ce que tu connais, outre les pianos,*
> *Le sobre et vespéral mystère hebdomadaire*
> *Des statistiques sanitaires*
> *Dans les journaux?)*

[But, woollens, mackintoshes, chemists, dream, curtains drawn on the waterfront balconies before the ocean of suburban roofs, lamps, prints, tea, petits-fours, will you be my only loves! . . . (Oh! and then, do you know, as well as the pianos, the sober vesperal weekly mystery of the health statistics in the papers?)]

Running through this tissue of interrelated images of dying nature and depressed human creation is the cry of the hunting horn, signifying man 'at bay'; the '*hallali*', signal to kill, is death closing in on him:

> *Et les cors lui sonnent!*
> *Qu'il revienne . . .*
> *Qu'il revienne à lui!*
> *Taïaut! Taïaut! et hallali!*

[And the horns ring out to it! Let it come back! . . . Let it come back! Tally-ho! Tally-ho! and in for the kill!]

But the voice of the horn is also repetition, the echo:

> *Les cors, les cors, les cors—mélancoliques! . . .*
> *Mélancoliques! . . .*

S'en vont changeant de ton,
Changeant de ton et de musique,
Ton ton, ton taine, ton ton! . . .
Les cors, les cors, les cors! . . .
S'en sont allés au vent du Nord.

[The horns, the horns, the horns—melancholy! . . . Melancholy! . . . go away changing tone, changing tone and music, tarra, tiree, tarra! . . . the horns, the horns, the horns . . . have gone away to the north wind.]

Just as there is repetition in the meaningless ritual of everyday middle-class existence as it impinges on the images of the poem—piano practice, the 'health statistics' in the newspapers—so everything within experience is a series of repetitions. Hence the fragmentation of themes and images, and their recurrence at several places within the single poem. Hence, above all, the haunting repetitions, not just in the references to the hunting horns but in minor images too. And, within the structure of the repetitions, alliteration, assonance and rhyme become a form of insistent musical repetition. Ultimately nothing is described; a balance between fragmentary concrete images and personal symbols, between physical perceptions, memories and associations, is set up, placing the total experience outside the constrictions of particular time or space. It is the onset of winter, the end of life, the end of hope, as transmuted through the particular sensibilities of an individual consciousness. In poems such as this Laforgue undoubtedly achieves the symphonic dream of which he had earlier written. As the critic, Jacques Rivière, privately wrote of him: 'How fortunate for him that he died so young! For what could he have added to the *Last Verses,* in which he has given the definitive account of himself. He could scarcely find a more fitting form.'

Rimbaud

Arthur Rimbaud also saw in the self the necessary focus for

poetic attainment of new truth. Rimbaud's poetic credo is generally taken to be contained in two letters he wrote in 1871, at the
age of seventeen. In the second and longer he says: 'The first study
of the man who wants to be a poet is to know himself in his
entirety. He seeks out his soul, inspects it, tempts it, learns to
know it.' When the would-be poet has explored his inner self in
this way, he is in a position to expand his vision into new imaginative fields. Whereas Baudelaire is concerned with the re-interpretation of what is, in order to penetrate to a metaphysical
truth, Rimbaud sees the poet as literally creating a new reality
out of his visions. The effort to train the senses to perceive the
world in a different way will end in the perception of a different
world.

The beginning of this process can be seen in his poem 'The
Drunken Boat', written in 1871. Initially the drifting boat sails
onward under its own volition: '*Les fleuves m'ont laissé descendre où
je voulais*' [The rivers let me go down where I pleased], but eventually it becomes the plaything of other forces, '*. . . moi bateau
perdu sous les cheveux des anses/Jeté par l'ouragan dans l'éther sans
oiseau.*' [me a boat lost under the hair of the bays, tossed up by
the storm into the birdless ether.] It is the image of the poet
deliberately submitting himself to his wild and eventually uncontrollable voyage into the unknown. For the boat and the
poet alike, the initial experiences seem traditional enough:
'*Le tempête a béni mes éveils maritimes*' [The storm has given its
blessing to my sea awakening], but it gains gradually in hallucinatory quality: '*J'ai rêvé la nuit verte aux neiges éblouies/Baiser montant
aux yeux des mers avec lenteurs*'. [I have dreamt of the green night
with its dazzled snows a kiss rising to the eyes of the sea slowly.]
The conventional world has been left behind thematically. But as
yet there is no new poetic form to match the dreamlike experiences evoked.

Within a year Rimbaud had started work on his first cycle of
prose poems, *Illuminations*, and had achieved a formal freedom to

match the themes of rebellion and liberation with which his poems were now exclusively concerned. The visionary seascape of the later stanzas of 'The Drunken Boat' had retained a certain physical coherence. Now, in the overlapping images of urban and rural, land and sea, in 'After the Flood', 'Mystique', 'Dawn', 'Common Nocturne' and 'Promontory', the conventional limits of reality no longer apply. In Rimbaud's own phrase 'a puff of breath scatters the boundaries of the hearth'. These visions, often accompanied by images of the dawn to emphasise that they are a renewal of the world, are coupled with a sense of moral liberation. As creator of his new world, Rimbaud selects its moral perspective as well as its aesthetic. Hence the emphasis on 'O *my* Good! O *my* Beautiful' with which he begins 'Morning of Intoxication'; where he goes on to promise the suppression of conventional standards, 'the tree of good and evil' in order to introduce 'our own very pure love'. Though this symbol of new love may well stem specifically from his homosexual relationship with the poet Paul Verlaine, it is poetically a general image of total moral liberation.

The sense of exhilaration is not, of course, to be taken for a sense of permanent achievement. In 'Vigils' there is a temporary hesitation, a sense of stasis akin to Baudelairean *ennui* in its neutral quality, and raising the same doubting question:

> *C'est le repos éclairé, ni fièvre ni langueur, sur le lit ou sur le pré.*
> *C'est l'ami ni ardent ni faible. L'ami.*
> *C'est l'aimée ni tourmentante ni tourmentée. L'aimée.*
> *L'air et le monde point cherchés. La vie.*
> *—Etait-ce donc ceci?*
> *—Et le rêve fraîchit.*

[It is rest in light, neither fever nor listlessness, in bed or in the meadow. It is the friend neither passionate nor weak. The friend. It is the beloved neither torturing nor tortured. The beloved. The air and the world not sought for. Life.—Is this then what it was?—And the dream grows cool.]

But the hesitation is temporary. The contemplation of reality stimulates, if only just, a dream state which in turn sets the creative process of imagination to work again. Equally, temporary setbacks are not to be taken for permanent failure. The important thing for Rimbaud in *Illuminations* is that the possibility of new experience is ever-present to the man who is master of his own imagination, and can invoke the magical powers inherent in language itself. As he expresses it in 'Clearance Sale':

Les Voix reconstituées; l'éveil fraternêl de toutes les énergies chorales et orchestrales et leurs applications instantanées; l'occasion, unique, de dégager nos sens!
　　A vendre les corps sans prix, hors de toute race, de tout monde, de tout sexe, de toute descendance! Les richesses jaillissant à chaque démarche! Solde de diamants sans contrôle!

[Voices reconstituted; the brotherly awakening of all energies in chorus and orchestrated and their immediate application; the occasion, a unique one, to liberate our senses! For sale bodies beyond price, such as are not found in any race, world, sex or genealogy! A fountain of riches at every step! Diamonds for sale, no quota!]

Yet by April 1873 this whole sense of the exploratory potential of the poetic imagination has begun to evaporate. *Une Saison en Enfer*, written between April and August of that year, not only accepts the failure of his attempt to defeat convention single-handed, it also denies the validity of his poetic approach. In the section 'Delirium II', subtitled 'Alchemy of the Word', he criticises his substitution of dream for reality, on the grounds that having reached the point of regarding his 'mental disorder' as sacred the habit of hallucination became a substitute for action. The self-criticism is, however, in no sense a sign of acceptance, either moral or aesthetic, of the old world. On the contrary, he rejects everything that contemporary society stands for. But it is *his* culture, and he admits that he cannot free himself totally from it:

I believe I am in hell, therefore I am there. It is the carrying out of the catechism. I am the slave of my baptism. Parents, you are the cause of my misfortune and the cause of your own. Poor innocent! —Hell cannot touch pagans.

The only way out of the impasse was silence, and escape into a life of action. Rimbaud appears to have written no more poetry after 1874. The last part of his short life was expended on travel, adventuring and finally trading in Africa. The vision, ultimately, proved valid for the self alone.

Mallarmé and the symbolists

From Nerval to Laforgue the poet-seers are working very much on their own, though they may share individual aspects of their private philosophies with other contemporary writers. But, with the collapse of the material certainties on which the Second Empire was based, there was in addition to the tendency to lapse into individual pessimism a substantial spread in idealist doctrines. This, in turn, led to the paradoxical appearance of a school of poetic visionaries, dedicated to achieving metaphysical certainties without sacrificing the role of individual experience or individual aesthetic sensibility. The metaphysical background to the symbolists, as the movement came to be known, derived almost exclusively from German idealist philosophy. As early as 1816–19 Victor Cousin had lectured on Kant, and both eclectic and— ironically—positivist philosophers had continued to translate and comment upon the works of Fichte, Schelling, Hegel and, belatedly, Schopenhauer. In practice the writers of the 1880s mostly knew very little of the specific doctrines of these thinkers, and it was on highly selective and at times inaccurate elements of their thought that individual symbolists built up their own beliefs. Of these, the fundamental one was that phenomena external to the self exist only in terms of the idea that the self creates of them (cf Laforgue). As Villiers de l'Isle-Adam expressed it in *Axel*: 'Know once and for all that there is no other universe for you than the conception of it reflected at the bottom of your thoughts, for you cannot see it fully, or know it, or distinguish a single point in it such that this mysterious point must be real in its reality.' The appeal of such a doctrine seems to have been that it justified the multiplicity of styles and interpretations exploited by writers, since each could claim a different vision. It is, in fact, a combination of Laforgue's view of the material world (without his belief in the unconscious) and Rimbaud's belief in the creative power of language; it is not a coherent philosophical position at all.

However, there is no doubt that the high priest of the movement, Stéphane Mallarmé, was genuinely concerned with metaphysical issues. From his earliest adult life he had experienced that familiar nineteenth-century sense that some transcendent reality lay beyond his grasp, which he could glimpse elusively through the shifting surfaces of the contingent 'real' world. In a relatively early poem, 'The Blue' (1864), the idea is overtly expressed. Haunted by eternity as symbolised in the blue of the sky, the poet curses his own poetic gift. For in granting him awareness not vouchsafed to his fellows, it seems only to endow him with the sterile possibilities of self-torment. He tries to escape by invoking the distractions of the material world, images of fog, muddied water and smoke. At the very moment when he seems to attain forgetfulness of the cruel ideal and approaches 'the litter where the happy brood of mankind is laid', he realises the impossibility of suppressing his special perceptions: '*En vain! l'Azur triomphe, et je l'entends qui chante/ Dans les cloches.*' [Vainly. The Blue is victorious, and I hear it singing in the voice of the bells.]

While attempting to achieve some metaphysical certainty—to break through the window and make contact with the sunset beyond, to use his own image from 'Windows'—Mallarmé underwent a spiritual crisis. There had always been, at the back of his mind, the fear that the search for the ideal might land him in precisely this predicament. In 'Windows' the flight into the sunset would be taken 'at the risk of falling for all eternity'. In 'Sea Breeze' the Baudelairean escape across unknown seas—the 'steamer with masts-a-sway setting out for an exotic landscape'—is interrupted by the sudden sense of potential shipwreck:

> *Et, peut-être, les mâts, invitant les orages*
> *Sont-ils de ceux qu'un vent penche sur les naufrages*
> *Perdus, sans mâts, sans mâts, ni fertiles îlots . . .*

[And, perhaps, the masts inviting the storms are among those that a wind bends above shipwrecks, lost, without masts, without masts, or fertile islets . . .]

The initial result of the crisis was to rob him of all sense of the meaningfulness of existence. But in the place of a conventional metaphysical solution he came to the conclusion that the negation of his personal significance gave a new significance to the products of his mind. He accepts death at one level in order to assert rebirth at another—as symbolised in the sonnet 'When the shadow threatened . . .' of 1874. For the world of literature, born of the writer's imagination and fixed in the creative medium of language, is unassailable by the forces of chance. It eternally reflects the consciousness of which it was the product. There is no need for this consciousness to mirror the world around it, for the inner world of dream and the contingent world of conventional reality are equally transitory until the creative act has moulded them into a permanent independent reality. The normal sequence of values is reversed, and a meaning for life can only be found in art. The idea receives repeated theoretical exposition in letters and articles from 1867 onward: 'Only Beauty exists, and it has only one perfect form of expression, Poetry. Everything else is delusion' (1867); 'Poetry is the expression of the mystery of existence, via language reduced to its essential rhythm: in this way it gives an authenticity to our existence and constitutes the only spiritual task' (1884); 'Everything in the world exists in order to end up as a book'(1891).

Once this position has been formulated philosophically, the only significant advances to be made were aesthetic. Mallarmé had early come to the conclusion that poetic communication depended upon evocation, not description; it was necessary 'to paint not the thing itself but the effect that it produces'. As he came to envisage the poet not as communicator but self-creator, this inadequacy of words to describe in a meaningful way became more important in proportion to the new subject matter of art. Verse itself—or poetic diction and structure, if the term 'verse' would seem to exclude prose-poetry—must remedy the inadequacies of conventional language, blending words without the usual restrictions of syntax and versification. It was here that Mallarmé came up against his last and unsolved problem, tormentedly expressed in the eccentric 'A Dice-throw will never Abolish Chance', where the typographical arrangement of the words mirrors the subject. The poet in his pursuit of the absolute via literature possesses only relative mastery of expression. In the process of selection involved in poetic composition, the poet is entirely subject to the hazard of intermittent inspiration: 'Every Thought gives off a throw of the Dice'. The exclusion of the random factor necessary if the poet is to ensure attainment of perfection is impossible because that factor is built into the relationship between mind and language.

In practice Mallarmé produced very little: the single volume of *Poèmes* published in 1887, three fragments of a planned dramatic work, *Hérodias*, and a handful of prose poems—that peculiarly French genre, to the foreign eye indistinguishable from poetic prose. Much of this work reflects the progression of his spiritual crisis; many poems are structured upon images of life, annihilation and rebirth, particularly oppositions of dark and light, sterility and creativity, cold and heat. Only one symbol takes on an almost fixed significance: the constellation of stars—the *septuor* of 'Its pure nails . . .' and the constellation itself of 'A Dice-throw . . .'— which represents the new world created by the poem. Even where one may speak of a fixed centre to the poems, there is no fixed meaning to the collocations of individual images in the sense of a critically definable 'correct' interpretation. As Jean-Pierre Richard put it in his *L'Univers imaginaire de Mallarmé* (1962):

> Nothing is more elusive than these poems, whose sense seems to modify from one reading to another and which never instil in us the reassuring certainty of having really, definitively understood them. But this variability of meaning should precisely be recognised as the true sense of the poem ... All perspectives are equally fruitful and the main thing will always be to go on multiplying their number.

In the strict sense Mallarmé was a precursor of the symbolists proper, for the manifestoes of the 'school' from which the title was to be derived did not appear until 1885, when Jean Moréas took it upon himself to defend the new movement in two articles, the first in *Le Dix-neuvième Siècle*, the second in *Le Figaro*. The main tenets of Moréas's definition are self-explanatory:

> The enemy of didacticism, declamation, false sensibility and objective description, symbolist poetry seeks to clothe ideas in a form that can be felt, but which nonetheless is not an end in itself, yet, while serving as a vehicle for an idea, would itself remain subject. The idea in its turn should not let itself appear deprived of its external analogues; for the essential character of symbolic art consists in never going as far as the conception of the idea itself. As for phenomena, they are only the perceptible surfaces designed to represent their esoteric affinities with the primordial ideas ...

It was not until his *Pèlerin passionné* of 1891 that Moréas actually published a work that fitted his own definitions. Nothing could be much less Mallarméan. The collection abounds with evocations of people and places of past ages; to match the themes, there are imitations of French medieval and Renaissance poets in matters of language and imagery. The main-line symbolists were really a completely separate group from Moréas and his friends. They can be defined in terms of the young poets who, between 1884 and 1898, gathered together every Tuesday evening from nine o'clock to midnight at Mallarmé's apartment to listen to the pronouncements of the master. Foremost among them were Gustave Kahn, Henri de Régnier and Francis Vielé-Griffin, joined from 1890 onwards by admirers younger still, notably Paul Valéry and André Gide. The very fact that the best definition of symbolism as a movement is a biographical one of this sort emphasises the absence of cohesion on a literary plain between what these various writers were attempting to do. The concept of the over-riding validity of the individual vision liberated the poet from the restraints of conventional verse form and diction—that much can be granted as a uniting phenomenon. But there is precious little in the way of metaphysical perception in the poetry of Kahn, though *Palais nomades* (1887) features a Laforguian *ennui*. Nor is there any overt 'visionary' element in the 'mood poems' of Vielé-Griffin's *Joies* (1889), or even his *La Clarté de vie* (1897), with its grave sense of correspondences between the soul and nature.

Undoubtedly the most important attempt to harness the new aesthetic to the expression of metaphysical ideas was not carried out in poetry at all, but in the plays of Maurice Maeterlinck. The young Belgian writer was not the only symbolist dramatist; Villiers de l'Isle Adam wrote three plays: *Eleü*, *Morgane* and *Axël*, and Paul Claudel produced *Tête d'Or* and *La Ville*. Only Maeterlinck married the symbolist aesthetic to a viable dramatic form (Claudel's overtly Catholic plays fall outside our terms of reference here), at least in his masterpiece *Pelléas et Mélisande*. A play of his had already been publicly performed in 1891; this was *L'Intrus*, a study of waiting for death and as such an allegory of the human condition. In it Maeterlinck's philosophical position is clearly set out: man is like a blind person, living in perpetual shadow and granted only occasional intuitive insights into the forces, usually evil, to which he is subjected. *Les Sept Princesses*, also published in 1891, and *L'Aveugle*, performed at the end of the year, offered further allegories on the same beliefs. *Pelléas et Mélisande*, written in 1892 and performed the following year, is altogether a more substantial and subtle work. At one level the plot has an extremely conventional element: two brothers, Golaud and Pelleas, become enemies when the former rightly suspects the latter of falling in love with his wife, Melisande. But at another level the stage becomes the setting for a struggle between powers of darkness and light, in which the symbol of love, Melisande, is ironically also the bringer of death. Action in the play can be defined not in terms of the plot but as the process of interior drama whereby external, metaphysical forces intervene in the lives of the characters via their individual psyches. It is the growing process of love within the two 'unaware' characters, Pelleas and Melisande, coupled with the brooding sense that destined love is also destined death. The reagent is Golaud—jealousy, non-communication, non-comprehension—a role to which he too is destined. Accordingly the play relies on spasmodic revelation to the spectator of stages in the mental development of the characters, which builds up a particular sort of atmospheric tension.

This deeper level of the play is conveyed in part by symbols, in part by special use of language. Some of the symbols function in a conventional way. Melisande, while talking to Pelleas, accidentally drops into a fountain a ring Golaud had given her. The fountain, once shallow and clear, is suddenly deep and muddied, making it impossible to retrieve the ring. Melisande then unaccountably misleads her husband as to how and why she lost it. Here we have the communication to the audience of a break with her husband and a commitment to Pelleas, both as yet unformulated in Melisande's own mind. They are clear to the spectator because of the conventional values attached to a ring. Other symbols, not possessing such conventional associations, function in a more opaque and purely emotive way. They are not pointers, for their significance becomes clear only after the event. Thus Melisande's tumbling and uncontrollable hair in act III sc 2 betrays the desire of her soul for Pelleas, a desire of which neither is yet aware. Yet other elements of the metaphysical dimension of the play are conveyed by the peculiar form of dialogue. Characters are unable to communicate rationally, as though their thoughts are distracted by an instinctive awareness of the threat to them from supernatural forces. This leads to a sharp distinction between sorts of dialogue: there are words which accompany and explain the action, and there are others, often only half-formed phrases, which betray the 'more solemn and uninterrupted dialogue of a being and his destiny', as Maeterlinck puts it in his essay *The Tragic in the Everyday*. This second form of dialogue, essential to cultivating emotional receptivity in the audience, is studded with unfinished phrases, silences, repetitions and large numbers of impersonal expressions—as, for example, when Melisande loses the ring:

Mel Oh! . . .
Pel It has fallen?
Mel It has fallen into the water! . . .
Pel Where is it?
Mel I cannot see it going down . . .
Pel I think I see it shining . . .
Mel Where?
Pel There . . . There . . .
Mel Oh! how far from us it is! . . . no, no, that is not it . . . It is lost . . . There is nothing left but a great ring upon the surface of the water . . . What shall we do? . . . What shall we do now? . . .
Pel One should not get upset like this over a ring. It is nothing . . . perhaps we shall find it again. Perhaps we shall find another . . .
Mel No, no; we shall never find it again, we shall never find others either . . . Yet I thought I had it in my hands . . . I had already closed my hands, and it fell all the same . . . I threw it too high, in the direction of the sun . . .
Pel Come, come, we shall return another day . . . come, it is time. We may be found . . . Noon struck at the moment when the ring fell . . .

Mel   What shall we tell Golaud if he asks where it is?
Pel   The truth, the truth, the truth . . .

In this type of dialogue the superficial meaning of the words is clearly of less account than the sense of confusion and apparently unmotivated guilt which underlies them.

Such a method of constructing a play has significant theatrical implications. First, the characters are 'outside time and space', and cannot in a conventional psychological sense develop. With the exception of Golaud's jealousy and the final realisation of love in act IV sc 4, the growth of fear in the face of death is the closest to conscious emotion they experience. Second, the symbols both textual and visual (in the décor) must have the power to suggest the creeping paralysis by which death takes hold of the characters and makes them accept their destiny. Third, this in turn, in terms of acting techniques, requires the elimination of the actor as a creative force, since any interpretation by him would only limit in some direction the spectator's right to choose a given value for a given symbol. Maeterlinck writes of his plays as 'marionette plays', not in the literal sense but to indicate how far his characters are puppets manipulated by destiny. He also says: 'Every masterpiece is a symbol, and a symbol can never tolerate the active presence of the man moving within it', conjecturing that he would be able to communicate more satisfactorily with the audience if the actors could be done away with altogether. For then the entire response of the spectator would be channelled into the creative reaction of his own intuitive processes.

Clearly there are limitations to *Pelléas et Mélisande* as a theatrical experience. To an astonishing degree it foreshadows modern anti-theatre—eg, Samuel Beckett—and is in that sense close to a denial of theatre as an art form. It is also impossible within Maeterlinck's formula to explore positive statements. That is why his later plays tended to be overtly allegorical, as with the popular *L'Oiseau bleu*, where Light is an active character, the bluebird symbolises knowledge, Tyltyl and Mytyl are the incarnation of childish innocence, and so on. Nonetheless, *Pelléas and Mélisande* is the only play of its generation to create a viable theatrical experience out of the interplay of the symbols themselves, while retaining the importance of its metaphysical dimension. If the play has faded from the modern repertoire, it is largely because it has been over-shadowed by Debussy's opera. Debussy had been in the audience at the play's private first performance and found in it the quality of text for which he had been searching for three years—where it would be the task of the music to underline the unexpressed and help to communicate what in the play was left to the eloquence of silence. The music also has the advantage that by introducing fragmentary, fugitive and unobtrusive *leit-motivs* associated with abstract concepts, such as remoteness, destiny and the awakening of love, the dramatic progression of the atmospheric structure can be enhanced in a way which the verbal text alone cannot achieve. Because of a quarrel as to whose mistress should sing the leading role, Maeterlinck did not consent to attend the original concert performance, but when he eventually saw the opera in 1920, ten years after Debussy's death, he is reported to have said: 'For the first time I have entirely understood my own play.'

From Nerval to Maeterlinck is a long voyage, and one which marks the extent to which symbolism, though it can be seen as the natural development of the tendency to seek within subjective inner reality a visionary insight into absolute truths, was also the clear end to such a line of exploration. Symbolism came perilously near to solipsism and silence. Yeats, in Ireland, Rilke and Stefan George in Germany, Volynsky and Bely in Russia, all continued the tradition. But, in France, Gide and Valéry, though their experience as disciples of Mallarmé was essential to their development, were to explore the self in rather different ways, reasserting the value of intellect. And for others the time had come to turn their backs on the self altogether and seek new collective values. Before we examine this reaction, there is one more field of subjective reality that stimulates substantial creative expression and is concurrent with the explorations of the visionaries. It affected those artists who, acknowledging no significant forces outside themselves, were content with heightening the experience of the moment.

THE AESTHETIC PURSUIT OF SENSATION

It may seem unfair to take the 'art for art's sake' movement as a starting point for the discussion of the pursuit of sensation. For Gautier, its leader and most successful practitioner, always held as his aim 'the form of beauty in its ideal state', and constantly speaks of the mystical nature of this ultimate ideal. Yet Baudelaire, when he observes that a thing is moral because it is beautiful, and Leconte de Lisle, when he claims that beauty and truth are identifiable, are making claims which, if disputable, are clearly mirrored in the transcendental element of their poetry and its inseparability from the form and expression of what they write. Whereas, in the Gautier of *Mademoiselle de Maupin* and *Emaux et camées* it is difficult to find more than a celebration of aesthetic pleasure in itself. As Carlyle puts it in *Sartor Resartus*: 'Even for the basest Sensualist, what is Sense but the implement of Fantasy, the vessel it drinks of?' And what is the pursuit of aesthetic pleasure but the enhancing through 'fantasy' of certain sense experiences?

Mademoiselle de Maupin is a case in point. The complicated and yet strangely absent plot revolves around the spiritual dissatisfaction of d'Albert, and the love he conceives, against his will, for the strange young Theodore, who is also loved by d'Albert's mistress, Rosette. The ambivalent Theodore, a girl in disguise, ends by yielding to both her lovers—though not in the precise form that either would initially have supposed—then disappears. The metaphysical implications of the story pick up the theme of the impossibility of human fulfilment which is central to many of Gautier's *Contes fantastiques*. But much of the text is devoted to the worship of beauty at an extremely sensual level, to the analysis of the impression of beauty upon the self, and to the creation of patterns within the writing which are decoratively beautiful in their own right. D'Albert's analysis of his own predicament has nothing metaphysical in it:

> If a man combined supreme beauty with supreme strength, if he had the muscles of Hercules beneath the skin of Antonoüs, what more could he desire? I am sure that with those two qualities and the soul that I have, I should be emperor of the world in three years!

After his transfiguration by his love for Theodore, this essentially physical side to d'Albert is still well to the fore:

> My rebellious body refuses to recognise the supremacy of the soul, and my flesh has no desire to be mortified. I find the earth as beautiful as heaven, and I think that perfection of form is virtue. Spirituality is not my strong point. I prefer a statue to a ghost and mid-day to twilight. Three things please me—gold, marble, and purple: brightness, solidity and colour.

As Theodore says of him, he perpetually aspires towards the beautiful, 'towards material beauty only, it is true, but that is in itself a noble inclination, and enough to maintain him in the pure regions'. This sensuality of desire is matched by a sensuality of fulfilment in the almost lubricious climax to the story. In the words of Theodore's last letter:

> You desired me, you loved me, I was your ideal—well and good. I at once gave you what you were asking for; it was your own fault that you did not get it sooner. I acted as body to your dream with all the complaisance in the world.

The final impression is one in which the spiritual loss is much overshadowed by the moment of physical bliss that precedes it. D'Albert (and Rosette) have achieved as much as could reasonably be expected in this world.

The style, too, encourages the view that the immediacy of a beautiful object is an end in itself. Almost timeless in setting and action, the novel gains much of its charm from the ingenious parallels with *As You Like It* which, in the shape of a theatrical performance, forms a large section of the action, and is at the same time a commentary on the whole triangular relationship. Individual episodes are written up with various kinds of bravura: letter, narrative, formal dialogue all diversify the narrative structure. Reflection and action alternate to the same end. One passage of supreme artifice—the account d'Albert sends his old friend Sylvio of how he has fallen in love with what he takes to be a boy —is couched in a spiral of embarrassed confession and conceals the gender of the beloved until the very last word of the chapter. It is no mean feat in a gender-conscious language to manipulate the pronouns for an entire chapter in such a way that elision always disguises the vital him/her or some periphrasis helps to avoid the issue. It is hardly surprising that a sensualist such as Swinburne should have called it 'the most perfect and exquisite book of modern times'.

The ambiguity between idealist aim and sensual aesthetic achievement which marks *Mademoiselle de Maupin* is also present in many of the poems of *Emaux et Camées*. The trivia of life are given artistic justification in poems like 'After the Paper' or 'The Good Evening'; the cult of the artificial for its own sake provides the imagery of 'First Smile of Spring'; the perverse and mysterious lend a *frisson* to 'Contralto', 'Carmen' and '*Caerulei oculi*'. The very best poems, 'Symphony in White Major' and 'Variations on *The Carnival of Venice*' transpose the sensations created by aesthetic objects—if either the colour white or a piece of music can correctly be called an 'object'—on to a purely sensual plane. It comes, then, as no surprise that Gautier eventually came to defend publicly the concept of decadence—in the preface to the 1869 edition of Baudelaire's *Fleurs de Mal*—or that he identified himself with decadent attitudes: the sense of pointlessness of life as it is normally lived, the desire to heighten the individual moment, the search for subtle forms of escape. Nor is it surprising that Gautier had a substantial influence on English decadents from Swinburne to Oscar Wilde, for in England aestheticism and decadence went hand in hand. With Gautier, we see, in fact, the establishment of what is an ever-widening phenomenon in nine-teenth-century French literature, the appeal to the immediate in the name of the pursuit of the infinite.

Seen in these terms Gautier has something in common with the Flaubert of the non-realist works, particularly *Salammbô*. The Flaubert who could write: 'I am convinced that the most frantic material appetites are unconsciously formed by bursts of idealism . . . ' is the author who projects on to the dream-world of *Salammbô*, unhistorical for all its documentation of ancient Carthage, the indulgence of vast sensual excess—gluttony, sadism, sexuality—all to the end of creating a work self-sufficiently beautiful. But, though Gautier is the forerunner of the 'sensualist' tradition, the nineteenth-century high-point of literature in which sense experi-ences are enjoyed for their own sake lies not in the 'self-conscious aesthete' manner but in the poetry of Paul Verlaine. His first col-lection, *Poèmes saturniens*, is a mishmash of different themes and styles, pastiching elders and contemporaries from Hugo to Baudelaire. It is blessed with an almost comically austere Parnas-sian prologue, which is studded with classical and oriental referen-ces, and proclaims the virtues of the poet-teacher who pursues a distant ideal of beauty while disdaining the crowd. However, some of the soulscapes of the section 'Sad Landscapes'—'Setting Suns', 'Twilight of the Mystic Evening' and 'Autumn Song'—already suggest, in their images of cradling, of drowning the senses, of drifting on the wind, the passive sensual receptivity of later works.

The next major work, *Fêtes galantes*, shows a definite develop-ment. This loosely structured cycle of poems uses the conventions of artistic transposition, dear to Gautier in his collection *España*, to recreate a series of moods via the filter of eighteenth-century painting, and its evocation in the Goncourt brothers' *Intimate Portraits of the Eighteenth Century* (1857) and *Eighteenth-century Art*

(1860). The tone is set by the opening poem 'Clair de lune' (Moonlight), where Verlaine projects his own soul as a landscape in which frivolity and sadness are complementary characteristics. Across the 'stage' of the collection flit the characters of the *commedia dell arte*—Pierrot, Harlequin, Colombine, Scaramouche, Pulcinella, *'l'excellent docteur Bolonais'*; through the shadowy, moonlit décor wander marquis and marquise, chevalier and abbé, all intent on the pursuit of self-gratification but betraying under their surface of pose and game, with its constant sense of cruelty, a void which becomes more evident as the collection progresses. Love is a constant war between the two sexes, in which the highest aim is to isolate the pure sensation of pleasure, and avoid the melancholy that may follow, or the dangers of emotional commitment. Yet languor and reverie, the vehicles of melancholy, are always in the background, and gradually absorb the consciousness of the characters. In 'Muted', the lovers have almost lost their identity as they submit to that passivity which seems their only way to escape responsibility for the self. The melancholy has to be voiced for them by the nightingale, so totally abstracted from the possibility of action have they become. And in 'Sentimental Conversation' they are true phantoms in whom the very experience of ecstasy has faded, the past made one with the present in its nullity:

> —*Te souvient-il de notre extase ancienne?*
> —*Pourquoi voulez-vous donc qu'il m'en souvienne?*

[Do you remember our former ecstasy? Why do you want me to remember it?]

After the disparate *La Bonne Chanson*, in which delicate verse of the *Fêtes galantes* type is largely submerged in prosaic poems of a rather self-conscious positive jollity, Verlaine perfected his evocative style in *Romances sans paroles*, written in 1871–2, though not published until 1874. It is the period of his affair with Rimbaud, who doubtless had an influence on the evolution of Verlaine's poetic manner. But the relationship is not overtly referred to in the major section of the work—the 'Ariettes oubliées'—for the good reason that it contains no clearly identifiable reference to any concrete experience. The assumption of passivity witnessed in 'Muted' has been metamorphosed into a total response to life. In these nine fragile poems, there is only one certainty, the absence of a conventional moral consciousness, even of any commitment to identify the nature of sense experience as the poet receives it. The person behind the poems is bewildered and childlike, accepting the world as a distant dream which is communicating with him through a haze:

> *Je devine à travers un murmure*
> *Le contour subtil des voix anciennes.*

[I guess through a murmur the subtle contour of voices of old.]

The poems are full of questions unanswered, of images of rocking, swinging, lulling, of childlike innocence:

> *Soyons deux enfants, soyons deux jeunes filles*
> *Éprises de rien et de tout étonées*
> *Qui s'en vont pâlir sous les chastes charmilles*
> *Sans même savoir qu'elles sont pardonées.*

[Let us be two children, let us be two little girls our fancy taken by nothing and astonished by everything who go off and grow pale beneath the chaste bowers without even knowing that they have been forgiven.]

To match the intangible subject matter, Verlaine has developed a complex poetic technique by which the reader's rational response is totally disorientated. In 'The piano that a frail hand kisses . . .', for example, the imprecision of the images is matched by syntactic and semantic ambiguities; the vocabulary lays stress on indefinites; colours and movements are muted, and at the same time enormous play is made with musical patterns that exist for their own value. The combined effect is to lull the reader into the same sense of helpless, distracted passivity. He is on the receiving end of an experience, a memory, a series of images, entailing music, dim colours, still movement, but in which all identity has been etiolated away to the point where the very nature of the experience is no longer certain.

The 'Ariettes oubliées' express in an extreme form the right of the self merely to experience the world without admitting responsibility towards it. Though some of the poems of *Paysages belges* exploit the same techniques in a less melancholy way, it was not a position capable of development, because the range of perceptions that could be expressed was by definition very limited. Hence the return, in other parts of *Romances sans paroles*, to the flat poetry of statement for which Verlaine had shown a weakness in *La Bonne Chanson*. His conversion to Catholicism and the collection of poems associated with it, *Sagesse*, foster this tendency still further, but, surprisingly, do not exclude the poetry of immediate sensation. For—like the poems of Dowson, his English Catholic equivalent—the greater part of the collection is not religious in a meaningful sense. Verlaine has merely accommodated his moral non-responsibility to the symbol of Mother Church and the Virgin Mary: '*Je ne veux plus aimer que ma mère Marie*' [I no longer want to love anyone but my mother Mary], and has sought to escape into the aesthetic charms of Catholic ritual and architecture, the 'vast and delicate Middle Ages' which he, significantly, prefers to the self-discipline of the 'jansenist' seventeenth century. Within the arms of this dual mother-figure, the child Verlaine is again rocked and soothed:

> *Je suis un berceau*
> *Qu'une main balance*
> *Au creux d'un caveau*

[I am a cradle rocked by a hand in the hollow of a burial-vault.]

At the same time he is free to indulge in the *frisson* of reliving his old sins through the filter of his repentance, so that memories take on the extra savour of forbidden fruit. It is a collection marked by a Swinburnian pleasure in pain, symbolised in the very first poem by the *chevalier* Misfortune who probes the poet's spiritual wound with the finger of his iron gauntlet; but the ambiguous experience is undergone in the surety that moral responsibility has been transferred to Mother Church.

With his '*Ars poetica*', written in 1874 but published in 1882, and the famous sonnet 'Languor' (1883)—'*Je suis l'Empire à la fin de la décadence*' [I am the Empire at the end of its decadence]— Verlaine finally dedicated himself to the cult of immediate sensation, although both poems merely refer to tendencies well established earlier in his work. The '*Ars poetica*' celebrates the aesthetic of the beautiful moment, the musical cadence savoured for itself alone; 'Languor' plays on the sense of solitude, *ennui* and moral impotence fundamental to the 'Ariettes oubliées'. If there is no philosophising in explicit terms, there is still the assumption that only the self has importance, and that the function of poetry is to preserve moments of extreme sensation and unique impression, using whatever elements of theme, imagery, language and verse form seem necessary, without regard for convention or propriety. It was this assumption of the pre-eminence of life as experienced by the individual self that made Verlaine dear to the young decadents to whose periodicals he contributed occasional poems over the period 1883–8. But, ironically, his own contribution to that style of thought and expression was almost played out. *Amour* (1888) and *Parallèlement* (1889) are marred by a wearisome explicitness only occasionally relieved by the erotic fervour that informs, for example, 'Those Passions', in the latter collection. From then on, until his death, Verlaine wrote nothing of significance, although he published much. From the cult of the senses in verse, he passed to the cult of the senses in real life—though there too the stimulus of his relationship with Rimbaud was apparently never regained—and his artistic creativity came to an end.

What Verlaine achieved in poetry, it was the task of Joris-Karl Huysmans to achieve in prose. In *A Rebours*, the bible of a generation, the hero, Des Esseintes, lives through the Baudelairian voyage of experience without the transcendental vision that gives the repeated renewal of the journey its significance. In the early novels, from *Marthe* to *A Vau-l'eau*, the oscillation of human experience between pain and boredom had formed the atmospheric background to a naturalistic treatment of contemporary urban life. In *A Rebours* this oscillation becomes the substance of the novel. There is no plot in the conventional sense. Des Esseintes, at the outset, has exhausted the customary pleasures of the world, finding that in every area of experience satiety is followed by lethargy and *ennui*. He therefore withdraws into an artificial world created for himself, by himself, in which to explore himself. Outside stimuli have become irrelevant to a mind so far advanced in its condition of neurasthenia that it can hallucinate at will:

> The essential is to know how to set about it, to know how to concentrate one's mind on a single point, to know how to abstract oneself sufficiently to bring on the hallucination and to substitute the dream of reality for reality itself.

Carefully Des Esseintes arranges his new house to reflect and advance his psychological condition. The very notion of the voyage is provided for in the dining-room, designed to give the illusion of the cabin of a boat. Lighting, smells, décor, everything creates the sensation of travel, without its distractions:

> In this way he procured for himself, without stirring, the swift, almost instantaneous, sensations of a long voyage, and this pleasure in travelling, which only exists in one's memory in fact, and hardly ever in the reality of the present, at the moment when it is taking place, he could drink in at his ease, without exhaustion, without fuss and bother, in this cabin whose carefully arranged disorder, whose air of transitoriness and temporary installation, corresponded more or less exactly to the temporary stay that he made there during the limited time he expended on his meals.

Each experience that Des Esseintes tries—the study of the Latin language and literature in the long period of 'decline' from Lucan to the Middle Ages; the cultivation of exotic hot-house plants; the contemplation of works of art, particularly those of Odilon Redon and Moreau—increases the physiological symptoms of his neur-asthenia. He is caught in the circular situation of needing, in order to give his mental existence significance, a psychological existence that destroys him physically. Music, modern literature (especially Mallarmé), religion as an aesthetic, not a spiritual, experience—the deeper he plunges into aesthetic satisfaction, the sicker he becomes. Finally medical advice makes it clear that he has a choice between returning to 'normal' life or continuing on into madness. In despair he accepts the former, while feeling that he is henceforth mentally dead since, without the self-creation of his cultivation of sense experience, his existence is merely a physical convention. Rather like Oscar Wilde's poem *The Sphinx* (1894), the novel ends on the cry of the unbeliever for whom only faith would create a meaning:

> Lord, take pity on the doubting Christian, on the unbeliever who would like to believe, on life's convict embarking alone, by night, beneath a firmament no longer lit by the consoling lanterns of the old hope.

As *Romances sans paroles* did for Verlaine, so *A Rebours* con-stituted for Huysmans the limits of both an approach to the world and an aesthetic credo. As with Verlaine, too, the next step was conversion to Catholicism, a conversion stimulated by the aes-thetics of religion and the fascination of the sense of sin, as *La Cathédrale*, *Là-bas* and *En Route* testify. But, unlike Verlaine, how-ever unconventional was the impetus towards the spiritual, Huysmans manifests no lapse into sensuality. With *A Rebours*, the self as sensualist and the aesthetic pursuit of sensation reach the conclusion of their nineteenth-century development—unless, that is, one sees in symbolism the apotheosis of decadence. For Des Esseintes acutely analyses in Mallarmé the self-deception of the idealist element:

In fact, the decadence of a literature irremediably attacked in its organism, weakened by the senility of its ideas, exhausted by the excesses of syntax, only responsive to the curiosities that make the sick feverish and yet in a hurry to express everything in the moment of its decline, determined on wanting to make good all the omissions of pleasure, to leave on its death-bed the most subtle memories of pain, this decadence was incarnated in Mallarmé in the most consummate and exquisite fashion.

Mallarmé should have been deeply distressed by such a reading of his work; but his poem, 'Prose for Des Esseintes', shows the very opposite response. Perhaps it was, after all, in *A Dice-throw will never Abolish Chance* that the cultivation of the aesthetic *frisson* reached its natural conclusion.

CHAPTER 4

Collective Values

Alongside the final flowering of subjective vision which characterises the symbolist movement, and with it all the major poetry of the last fifteen years of the nineteenth century, there arose a directly contrary movement devoted to the reinstatement of collective values. Its two constituent elements, concurrent and often overlapping—but not identical—phenomena during the period 1890–1918, were the Catholic revival and the rise of nationalism. Both have their roots in the intellectual and political disarray of the early Third Republic, but it was primarily to counter intellectual individualism that the Catholic movement developed, whereas the nationalist movement drew principally on social discontent.

INTELLECTUAL BANKRUPTCY AND THE CATHOLIC REVIVAL

By the fall of the Second Empire in 1871, positivism had enjoyed twenty years and more as the almost unchallenged philosophical basis to intellectual activity. It had evolved under Renan, and was to continue to evolve under Taine, from a methodology into a thoroughgoing religion, with its promises of the perfecting that human nature would undergo through the benign influence of science. By the 1880s the shortcomings of such a philosophy as a view of life had become only too clear to a substantial number of the younger generation, on three counts. Firstly, as Claude Bernard had warned, it too rigidly excluded that metaphysical dimension which is fundamental to man, especially in youth. Secondly, positivism seemed to condone the materialist excesses of the upper and middle classes—excesses no less in the early Third Republic than under Napoleon III. Thirdly, it suffered the fate of eighteenth-century rationalism; the traumatic experiences of the Franco-Prussian War and the Paris Commune (1871) discredited the claim that any permanent amelioration of human nature was under way. Since positivism was taken as synonymous with rationalism and science, mistrust for all application of reason and for all systematic inquiry was fundamental to the reaction against it. Such a mistrust rapidly developed into whosesale anti-intellectualism.

At the same time there was a dissatisfaction with those who tried to find purely subjective alternatives to positivism. The literature of the 1870s and 1880s in particular suggested that the status given to the individual in German philosophy from Kant to Hartmann, and notably the special value attributed to the experience of the individual consciousness by Schopenhauer, led only to boredom, lassitude, a meaningless progression through experience, similar to that already chronicled by Baudelaire and which was to reach its peak in the torpid melancholy and neurasthenia of Huysmans' Des Esseintes and Laforgue's *Complaintes* (1885). Individualism led directly to decadence, be it the frivolous formalism of Théodore de Banville's later poetry or the hopeless exploration of each sense experience for its own sake, as in Verlaine's *Romance sans paroles*. Just as anti-rationalism became anti-intellectualism, so this anti-individualism crystallised into a call for order, hierarchy and collective responsibility. To combat the lethargy which characterised decadence, energy became a virtue in itself and, with it, extremism, for intellectual excess often stems from the release of superabundant energies in a particular cause.

The natural repository on both the metaphysical and the social

levels for these new-found energies was Catholicism. Individualism was automatically associated with Protestantism, not to men-
tion democracy and socialism—the Catholic Church could not be
accused of sympathy with any of the three. Partly through fear of
what happened to it in the aftermath of the Revolution, it was
firmly committed to social conservatism. It also had the advantage
of not having attracted any substantial literary adherents since
Chateaubriand, an advantage in the sense that to be Catholic and
an intellectual carried the cachet of originality. The revival was,
however, not only a new movement within society; it was also a
new movement within the Church. The proportion of ordinary
people who regarded themselves as practising Catholics was still
high—it is nonesense to regard Catholics as a minority at the
turn of the century, except perhaps in Paris itself—but religion
had become a very conventional affair. The Church took care not
to trouble the material ease of the *bourgeoisie,* and they in turn paid
token tribute to the moral hegemony of the Church. The hazy
amalgam of aestheticism and pantheism, which formed the
metaphysical link between Romantic Catholics and Christian
belief, had long ceased to have any serious proponents, leaving
transcendental issues to the theologians proper.

The major spur to a reaction against this state of affairs can be
seen in the proliferation of minor prophets and miracles that
occurred as the century progressed; of these, the Miracle of La
Salette in particular seems to have played a substantial
part in fashioning the religious sensibilities of writers of the
revival. In 1846 a peasant girl, Mélanie, had experienced a
vision of the Virgin; the full account of this, by divine order, was
not revealed until 1858. The message of the vision, and the cult
that grew up around it, stressed to the point of heresy all those
aspects of Catholic doctrine that were least represented, or even
neglected, in the official church of the day. The priesthood was
denounced for its weakness and corruption, the collapse of society
and the end of the world were predicted, and the need for repara-

tion for the sins of the world in general and the Church in particular was trumpeted forth in no uncertain terms. Expiation,
reparation, penitence were the catchwords, sinfulness and suffering ineluctably linked in a most unpleasant form of neo-medieval
self-immolation. Here was a focus for those who wanted to preserve their individuality (nothing stimulates the individual consciousness so well as a permanent submersion in mental and
physical pain) while subordinating themselves to the needs of a
corporate body, the Church, with a hierarchical, if imperfect, social
structure and an equally hierarchical, and unchallengeable, intellectual structure.

Accordingly, the writers of the Catholic revival came to stress
as the central features of religion all those aspects of doctrine
least in key with the society of the day and least accessible to the
ordinary unbeliever—or indeed believer! It is a notable fact
that every single major figure of the revival was a convert, whether
central to the movement, like Huysmans, Léon Bloy, Charles
Péguy and Paul Claudel, or peripheral to it, such as Francis
Jammes. Their approach was often eccentric: through aestheticism and occultism in the case of Huysmans; through mysticism
with a strong social admixture in the cases of Bloy, Péguy and
even Claudel.

However different their individual works, these writers tend to
share a number of basic beliefs none of which are central to
Christianity. Firstly, they completely discarded the use of intellect in religious matters; since religion was the key to the whole
of life, this meant for practical purposes that they discarded intellectual activity altogether. The one exception was Paul Bourget
(1852–1935), the critic and novelist, whose major work, from *Le
Disciple* (1889) onward, denounces and illustrates the evil effects
of materialism and nihilism, but attempts to offer a rational basis
for the Catholicism and extreme social conservatism which his
heroes espouse. In practice, it is true, Bourget uses reason to
destroy the arguments of his opponents and falls back on the doc-

trine of grace to explain the phenomenon of belief. In using rational argument he does admit a limited value to reason; not so his contemporaries. Yet aesthetically this leads to their superiority, for they are forced to develop emotive ways to communicate ideas and ideals emotively conceived, whereas Bourget's novels all lapse into a sterile didacticism. He is the one major Catholic writer of his period who is largely unread today. In place of reason the other writers championed revelation, and this in turn led them to stress the trappings of mysticism, the miraculous and visionary, as the physical reality of religion. Hence the fondness for La Salette, and the stress laid, particularly by Bloy, on the reality of the Second Coming. It was the simplicity of the peasant or, to put it less politely, the credulity of the simple-minded raised to the status of a substitute for intelligence. Secondly—and this the Catholic writers have in common with Bourget—they all subscribed to an extremely right-wing view of society, a view which was to remain important in *bien-pensant* circles well into the twentieth century, surfacing as the theoretical basis for the Vichy régime during World War II and having much in common with the social vision promoted by General de Gaulle under the Fifth Republic.

The most coherent exponent of a fixed social order relying upon the family unit and the social restraints of Christian virtue is Bourget, but the other writers betray much the same social assumptions. Péguy, with his early support for socialism, seems out on a limb, but he was eventually alienated by what he regarded as the excesses of the Combes government (1902–5) and fell back upon a vision of the devoted worker and his paternal overlord labouring happily together towards a Christian society—a vision which accepted, just as much as Bourget did, the natural inequality of man. Only Bloy espoused the cause of the socially underprivileged in a meaningful way; yet he was too obsessed with their spiritual needs to engage himself seriously with their material problems, for their sufferings seemed to him to their ultimate advantage. Such social doctrines were designed not so much to preserve the status quo—for the writers had no interest in the power of the *bourgeoisie*—as to return to an earlier state: they harked back to an idealised version of feudal society.

This *aperçu* of the social views of the Catholic revival brings us to its third common factor: the desire to escape into the past, almost without exception into the Middle Ages. The suffering and resurrection of France under Joan of Arc is a favourite symbol, as in Péguy's *Jeanne d'Arc* (1897) and *Mystère de la Charité de Jeanne d'Arc* (1910); Bloy's *Jeanne d'Arc et l'Allemagne* (1910), and in the political background to Claudel's *L'Annonce faite à Marie* (1912). Other holy figures without patriotic associations are also the source of inspiration—eg, in Huysmans' *Sainte Lydwine de Schiedam* (1901). Of the three aspects of the Middle Ages that typify this fascination, the least significant is the aesthetic. The debasement of popular religious art, particularly the pictorial, was a genuine source of distaste to people of cultural sensitivity. The Middle Ages had the virtue of combining great monuments to religious inspirations with solid theology and social order. Hence, in a certain measure, the fondness for the theme of the cathedral, as in Huysmans' *La Cathédrale* (1888), and the symbols of cathedral-building and the builder, Pierre de Craon, in Claudel's *L'Annonce faite à Marie*. The second aspect, social order, was derived from an idealisation of the Middle Ages as a period of faith, in which the Church was unblemished within and unchallenged without. Bloy's *La Femme pauvre* (1897) links these two aspects, order and aesthetics, when he describes the medieval Church as 'an immense church . . . a place of prayer as vast as the whole of Western Europe'. Sometimes this view is countered by the completely opposite one of the Middle Ages as a society completely corrupt and on the point of collapse, only to be resurrected by the force of religion (eg, St Joan), as in *L'Annonce faite à Marie*. In general, however, the feudal society at prayer is maintained as the model for the new Christian society that is to replace a contemporary society hopelessly corrupted by science and capitalism.

Perhaps more important still as a doctrine binding together the writers of the Catholic revival is the one tenet to which they all unflaggingly return, that of suffering for others in order that they may be relieved of the burden of their sins. This doctrine of vicarious suffering is a perfectly respectable aspect of orthodox Christian belief; a good Christian can, through prayer, self-denial and suffering, take on some of the burden of the sins of mankind in general, as Christ did upon the Cross. The sufferer is called by God to the task, and of his or her own will responds to the call, as was the case with Huysmans' Blessed Lydwine. The doctrine was much alluded to by the various minor prophets of the century and was central to the cult of La Salette. It became the cause of heresy in the tenets of the Abbé Boullan, whose spiritual teachings—but not the secret erotic excesses with which they were associated—considerably affected Huysmans and Bloy; for both these writers, vicarious suffering represented the ultimate in human experience. In Bloy's case, the portrait of suffering is in part identified with the fate of the poor, whom he equates with Christ; his insistence on its paramountcy is so violent as to indicate an unbalanced mentality. With Huysmans there is an element of sado-masochism strongly reminiscent of Swinburnian algolagnia:'Come down and redeem us from virtue, Our Lady of Pain'. The most creative use of the doctrine is made by Claudel. He retains the literal-mindedness with which his *confrères* picture the transference of sin; for, as with miracles, it is the externals that fascinate them as much as the spiritual values of which the outward manifestations are the symbols. From *L'Otage* (1909) onward, the doctrine, used firstly with a political significance, later in a more personal way, always appears in close association with the idea of the necessary separation of lovers. Yet, even in this more psychologically orientated form, the obsession with expiation, whether personal or social, individual or universal, remains for the unfanatical peculiarly unpalatable and inhuman.

These, then, are the aspects shared by the major writers of the revival. What of their individual achievements?

Joris-Karl Huysmans

After writing the breviary of decadence, *A Rebours*, Huysmans moved toward Catholicism via a study of satanism in *Là-bas* (1891). The major works of the post-conversion period still accessible to the modern reader are *En Route* (1895), *La Cathédrale* (1898) and *L'Oblat* (1903). In all three there is an insistence on the harshness and sacrifice necessary for true religion. Durtal, the hero of *Là-bas* and mouthpiece of the author, experiences while on retreat the severity and yet the calm spiritual achievement of Trappist monks (*En Route*); comes into contact with the penitential cult of La Salette, and enjoys the physical and spiritual benefits of Chartres Cathedral (*La Cathédrale*). He ends up, in the eponymous novel, as an oblate—a position akin to that of a monk but less closely tied by vows and spiritual restrictions—and falls victim, like the Benedictine monks to whom he is attached, to the wave of political anti-clericalism that followed the resolution of the Dreyfus affair. What the reader retains is not the sense of sin and expiation but the strong aesthetic sensitivity so reminiscent of that of Des Esseintes in *A Rebours*. Durtal's conversion is achieved via the ambiguous message of Grünewald's tortured painting of the sufferings of Christ; he explores the meaning and emotional power of architecture, plainsong and litany; he remains constantly aware of colour, texture and light. This is where the strength of the novels lies. Not without justification did Bloy, in *La Femme pauvre*, pillory Huysmans as a dilettante, in the character of Follantin— the name of the hero of Huysmans' own novel, *A Vau-l'eau* (1882).

Léon Bloy (1846–1917)

Bloy's works, *Le Désespéré* (1886), *La Femme pauvre* (1897) and his collection of short stories, *Sueur de sang* (1893), are utterly different in style and conception from those of Huysmans. In the short stories, which are a paean of hatred for Germany based on incidents from the Franco-Prussian war, a number of Bloy's ideas are clearly exposed: the sanctity of France as the elect nation of God, the purification which sinners can achieve for themselves by self-sacrifice in the cause of France, and the contemptible venality of the middle and upper classes who damn themselves in the interest of material comfort. In the novels the chaos of visionary beliefs is a deal more difficult to reduce to any kind of coherent system. *Le Désespéré* is a spiritual autobiography, in which the author projects himself into the character of Caïn Marchenoir—the very name has undertones of sin and suffering. The prostitute, Anne-Marie Roulé, with whom Bloy had a difficult relationship, becomes in the novel the religiously inspired ex-prostitute Véronique. Some episodes of the book are self-explicit, but so much of it is a *roman-à-clef*, and the explanation of the divine symbolism of history so eccentric that the work as a whole is hardly accessible to the modern reader.

La Femme pauvre, though it conceals a number of personal allegiances and hatreds, rests on a recognisable theological basis, the doctrine of various suffering. Clotilde, persecuted by her vile step-father, Chapuis, seduced and abandoned by a worthless lover, achieves material happiness through the help of the painter, Gacougnol, and intellectual enlightenment from his friend, Marchenoir. But, as Clotilde perceives in a visionary moment, her destiny is linked with Léopold, friend of the other two. Gacougnol dies, failing by seconds to complete the will which would have established Clotilde's future comfort, and his miserly bourgeois heir declines to give her any assistance. Her subsequent marriage to Léopold is marked by disaster, including the tragic loss of their child. All the time, the wretched couple are harassed by the forces of convention, representing all that is rotten in contemporary society—the supreme examples being the harpies, Mme Poulot and Mme Grand, who live opposite their suburban retreat.

Léopold's sight begins to fail, Marchenoir, their aid and comforter, dies, and the neighbours step up their insensate persecution to a demonic level. Finally, in a cry of anguish, Léopold offers up his life to God in exchange for the punishment of their tormentors:

> ... Without beating about the bush, what I am asking you for against those two women is a rigorous punishment such as to make Your name shine forth in all its glory, that is to say, a very clear punishment which will make their sin manifest. I ask you, finally, that this punishment should be soon ... Mark well, Lord Jesus, that what I am offering you is nothing less than my own life, in exchange for this act of justice, which I entreat with all the strength that Your Passion on the Cross has given to the prayers of mankind!

With an Old Testament simplicity the prayer is answered: one old woman is eaten by her own dog; the other goes mad. Léopold pays the price he has offered by dying in repeated attempts to save the lives of women and children in the terrible conflagration of the Opéra-Comique—this, one of the greatest catastrophes of the age, being transformed by Bloy into a God-sent punishment for the sins of the *bourgeoisie*. The novel closes with the portrait of Clotilde living out her days in devout poverty, having achieved a sense of earthly paradise: 'I am perfectly happy ... Paradise is not a place you enter tomorrow or the next day or in ten years time; you are in it today, if you are poor and crucified'.

Here is the key to the novel. Every form of earthly happiness Clotilde attains, however innocent, is taken from her. Material and intellectual well-being, the happiness of motherhood and wedlock are all acquired only to be tragically lost. But this process is God's will: 'Everything that happens is to be worshipped'. Her suffering saves and purifies her soul in a way inaccessible to the corrupt world around her—hence the constant visions, revelations, passages of scripture and, above all, the emphasis on suffering. In Clotilde's own words: 'Happy are they who suffer and weep.' As the articulatory force of Bloy's vision of the world, the doctrine, however repellent, lends immense artistic conviction to a novel in which the normal canons of psychological realism simply do not apply.

Charles Péguy (1873–1914)

Huysmans and Bloy seem to exhaust the two principal directions, aesthetic and visionary, which the novel could, at that period, take in the attempt to compel the reader's assent to Catholic truths. Péguy and Claudel sought to achieve the same effect through the renewal of other literary forms. In the case of Péguy, his attentions were divided between poetry and verse drama, on the one hand, and the prose commentary on current events written for his periodical, *Cahiers de la Quinzaine* (1900–14). Péguy was not so much a convert as a re-convert, but even in his non-Catholic writings of 1891–1905 there is very little that is not coherent with the explicitly religious works of the period 1910–14. The most consistent feature of Péguy's work is his anti-intellectualism. This hostility binds together his social and religious views, for the assumption of conventional knowledge causes the same barrier between intellectual and worker as between intellectual and God. Péguy had reached the heights of the French educational ladder, but left the École Normale prematurely, in revolt against the rationalism that prevailed there. His attack on the intellectual traditions of his day, particularly on Taine and Renan—though his account of the latter is not unsympathetic—is most clearly set out in *The Situation of the Intellectual Party in the Modern World* (1906). His arguments betray a classic case of the assumption, so common in his generation, that if the state of a society is not acceptable, the principles underlying it are at fault, not the way they have been put into practice. The opposite position, as propounded by Péguy, is one in which man puts himself totally in the hands of God, freely surrendering the right to think and act on his own account. For such a man earthly wisdom has only a distracting power.

The embodiment of simple faith which Péguy holds up to us is the peasant (one could compare G. M. Hopkins's 'Felix Randall'); here again his social and religious views closely overlap. His flirtation with socialism, though genuinely founded in a belief in the brotherhood of man—or at least of all Frenchmen—was based not on a coherent political interest in the workers but on a profound compassion for the poor. As early as 1902 his writings on poverty show that his concern was not with material equality but with the re-establishment of a moral unity which he felt had existed in the France of the Middle Ages. Hence the ease with which in later works he assimilates his social views to the feudalism of his fellow Catholic writers. Moreover, the passionate belief in the virtues of peasant simplicity also led to an easy assimilation of patriotism to faith. In *Notre Patrie* (1905) the sense of belonging to the soil and the willingness to fight for it are identified as peasant virtues. Through the image of Christ, as a fellow-peasant in the *Mystère de la Charité de Jeanne d'Arc*, Péguy arrived naturally at a vision of France as the chosen nation of God, fully akin to Léon Bloy's but not relying on the mystical Biblical exegesis which Bloy professed. For the Péguy of the *Mystère des Saints Innocents* 'faith is a church, a cathedral rooted in the soil of France'. Thus his severally championed causes combine to lead him to the embarrassing excesses of patriotic tub-thumping that mar his final poetic work, *Eve* (1913): 'Happy are those who have died for the fleshly earth/Provided their death was in a just war'. Perhaps it is not to be wondered at that a champion of medieval simplicity and faith should end his poetic career on a note of simple-minded dogmatism worthy of the *Song of Roland* (c AD 1100).

Paul Claudel (1868–1955)

Of the four major writers of the revival, the greatest by far is Claudel. One reason for this superiority is the experimentalism of his theatrical forms, whose literary richness was not destined to find a director capable of interpreting it in practical terms until the

1940s, a factor which makes Claudel, the dramatist, more a part of twentieth-century developments than of the period under review here. But his second claim to greatness is the clarity and coherence with which he blends the various aspects of his belief into a system. This he had already achieved in *L'Annonce faite à Marie* (1912), towards which all his early works, from *Tête d'or* (1890) to *L'Otage* (1911), present a clear evolution. The earliest plays seem primarily concerned with the destruction of the old order which must precede the spiritual renaissance of society. Their symbolism is not specifically religious, and indeed the opening theme of *Tête d'or*—a dying kingdom and a dying king who must be slaughtered by the man of will—Tête d'or himself—is a reflection of the Orphic cycle, in a form close to that propounded by Nietzsche. But already Claudel rejects the idea that a meaningful existence can be generated outside faith even by a man who has the strength of will to attempt the task; at the end of the play Tête d'or recognises the futility of his existence in the face of death. The message that can be derived from this and the following two plays, *La Ville* (1890) and *L'Echange* (1894), is composed of three elements which will remain essential to the later plays: first, hostility to materialist society and the need for its destruction —modified into the need to struggle to destroy its values; second, the need for faith in the rebuilding of the moral order; third, the value of suffering. Three further elements were to be added. The first is his Hopkins-like sense of joy in his new-found Christian belief, and the relief he felt at submitting himself entirely to what he saw as the will of God (unlike Hopkins in the 'terrible' last sonnets, Claudel had no difficulty in perceiving what the will of God was). These feelings are extremely important to the *Cinq Grandes Odes*, poems written in 1905–8 and published in 1910. The second element is his concept of human love, profoundly affected by the adulterous affair he contracted in 1900. The fruits of this unfortunate relationship can be seen in *Partage de midi* (1906) and constantly thereafter; lovers must be separated, their salvation derives from the ensuing suffering. Marriage, in contrast, has the function of imposing a discipline on man, a discipline sanctified by God. It creates the family, a fundamental social unit, and hence a necessary element of order. Marriage and love are therefore complementary, and their separation is necessary to both society and individual. The third and last element—the mystical patriotic view of France as the saviour of Christendom, already noted in Bloy and Péguy in different forms—first finds its definitive form in the historical background to *L'Annonce faite à Marie*, but was not the central theme of an individual work until *La Nuit de noël 1914* (1915).

In *L'Annonce faite à Marie* all these Claudelian themes— rejection of materialism, power of faith, virtue of suffering, separation of lovers, mystical significance of France—are brought together for the first time, and possibly to greater effect than in any later work. (The following analysis and discussion of the play are based on the final text, the acting edition of 1940; there are substantial but relatively unimportant differences between this and the original edition.) The plot is straightforward but dis-jointedly presented. In fact, the play is meaningless if defined in terms of plot alone, because it comprises a series of interrelated symbols, which include not only symbolic action but setting, character (even down to the very names) and elements of staging —eg, the periodic ringing of church bells. It is set in the Middle Ages. The heroine, Violaine, pardons with a symbolic kiss the stone-mason and leper, Pierre de Craon, who has attempted to rape her. Her father, Anne Vercors, departs on a pilgrimage to Jerusalem, for he despairs at the decayed state of France; he entrusts the estate of Combernon and the hand of Violaine to Jacques Hury, the man she loves. Mara, her sister, who also loves Jacques, and has seen the kiss given to Pierre without understand-ing its true meaning, tries to turn Jacques against his betrothed. Violaine of her own will renounces him, having realised that her vocation is to serve God and renounce the world. Her kissing of

Pierre has transmitted his leprosy to her, symbol of her isolation and of her acceptance of his sin. Jacques, uncomprehending, in turn renounces Violaine and marries Mara. The scene then shifts seven years. France and the Catholic faith have been saved, but Mara's only child is dead. She brings it to Violaine, who is by now in the last stages of the living death of leprosy but famous for her saintly works. The child is reborn—in the image of Violaine. Mara attempts to engineer her sister's death, but her father, returning from his pilgrimage to find the dying Violaine, understands all that has happened. As Violaine is received into the peace of God, her father interprets the events for the others.

The fundamental Catholic message within the play rests on the symbolic roles of the characters. The symbols are lyrical, not logical, and as such have a fluidity they would not have if they were strictly allegorised. Violaine, for example, in taking the sins of Pierre, her kin and the world on her shoulders, is a Christ figure. At the same time she is the Virgin Mary—giving birth to Mara's child—marked by God and obedient to him, as is explicit in the last scene of the play. Similarly, Anne Vercors is in a sense a God figure, as the exhibition of clemency at the opening of act I sc 3 suggests. Combernon without him is the world without God, paradise suddenly thrown into disorder. However, at the last supper before he leaves on his pilgrimage, with its cryptic references to an unspecified moment of return—'I shall return at the moment when you do not expect me'—he is clearly Christ. Yet, ultimately, he is merely human, testifying that Violaine, by simply staying at home and sacrificing herself, has achieved what he was trying to do, and failed, through his pilgrimage. Despite this extreme fluidity of symbolism, there is a simple symbolic scale against which all the characters can be measured. Violaine is the incarnation of the spiritual, the human embodiment of the values represented by the isolated convent of Monsanvierge, which stands above and apart from Combernon in the physical setting of the play. At the other end of the scale, Mara—her name betrays her nature: 'Call me not Naöme, that is *the beautiful*, but call me Mara, that is *the bitter*, because the Almighty has filled me brimfull with bitterness' (*Ruth* I:20)—is the incarnation of the material, and the human embodiment of the soil of Combernon. Anne Vercors is the midway mark, maintaining a precisely balanced relationship between the material and the spiritual, never failing in his duty towards the soil or towards God. Jacques, like Mara, is turned to the soil, and fails to comprehend his spiritual duties, whereas Pierre de Craon is turned towards the spirit. He understands that Violaine is marked out by God, because he himself is called to make a more minor sacrifice of the same order.

Within the action of the play there are certain major symbols. For example, Pierre's leprosy is the physical manifestation of a spiritual impurity. Violaine's kiss is therefore the voluntary acceptance of his sin, her first acceptance of vicarious suffering, and Pierre is healed. In the prologue, Violaine presents Pierre with the pagan ring which Jacques had given her, and thus renounces the profane world in general and Jacques in particular, the first act in the renunciation of physical experience. The major moments of the play—the 'last supper' (act I sc 3), the renunciation scene in the orchard (act II sc 3), the resurrection of Mara's child as the Christmas bells ring out and the triumphant procession of the new king passes (act III sc 2)— all feature symbolic acts of this kind. The politico-religious background to the play forms almost a symbolic sub-plot in itself. To give full value to Violaine's sacrifice and acceptance of the sins of others, Claudel has placed the play at a synthetic moment of time, when the social fabric is supposed to be crumbling and, with it, the basis of all political and religious institutions. The very deliberate symbolism of this is made clear from the first historical references in Anne Vercors' great speech in act I:

In the place of the King we have two children.
One, the Englishman, in his island,

And the other, so small he cannot be seen, among the reeds of the
Loire.
In the place of the Pope we have three of them, and in the place
of Rome some council in Switzerland.

The last decades of the English occupation of France, the period of
the Avignon popes, and the early Reformation are all made
contemporary, to stand for the essence of flux and decay: 'All is
struggle and movement'.

With this symbolism of action Claudel combines a symbolism
of setting. In terms of place, Combernon, a fruitful plain dominated by the convent of Monsanvierge, represents the subordination
of the material to the spiritual. In terms of time, the action is fulfilled within a cycle of seasons. The prologue and act I take place
in spring, associating spiritual preparation with the season of
growth; act II takes place in summer, so that the flowering of
Violaine's spiritual resolution accords with the season, and at the
same time her renunciation of the material world is the renunciation of a world at its most rich, luxuriant and attractive; act III
takes place in winter, the moment of Nietzschean total annihilation before rebirth—here the physical rebirth of France is secondary to the spiritual rebirth, birth being underlined by the fact
of the Nativity and the resurrection of Mara's child. Finally, act
IV, as the action comes to fruition, is set at the moment of the
earth's maturity, the early autumn.

The Catholic ethic at the centre of the play is plainly twofold.
Firstly, the pure soul is marked for God by the special gift of
grace. Though he or she has free will to accept or reject that gift,
the right path is to accept the role determined by God, and to renounce entirely all claims on the material world. As Pierre puts it
in the prologue:

Saintliness is not a matter of going and getting yourself stoned to
death by the Turks, or of kissing a leper on the mouth, but of carrying out God's orders at once, be they to stay in your place or to
ascend higher.

Secondly, God's chosen instrument can, by his or her suffering, redeem the sins of the world. From the outset Violaine advises Pierre that suffering is a consolation in itself. The physical regeneration of Pierre, of the child and of France are what her own suffering achieves. These two threads are drawn together and given full exposition in Anne Vercours's speech of act IV sc 2:

> Is the aim of life to live? Are the feet of God's children bound to this wretched earth?
> The aim is not to live but to die! Not to fashion the cross but to ascend it and give happily all we possess.

We are not offered Christ triumphant, but Christ in agony on the cross, as our pattern. The person who is marked out for such a role can by his renunciation of the world and his acceptance of pain redeem both those close to him and the human race in general. This is the ethic that binds the other themes—the separation of the lovers and the marriage of Jacques and Mara that seals that separation, the worth of inherited values, the power of faith, the renaissance of France itself—into a powerful exposition of the true Christian message as Claudel sees it.

The common features of the major writers of the Catholic revival fall, then, into two groups: their insistence on doctrinal issues, in particular the harsher and more mystical aspects of Catholic doctrine, and their strong views on the social issues of the day, particularly the need to reimpose a rigidly ordered, hierarchical structure in France. This combination of interests is less paradoxical than it might at first seem when we remember that it is the Middle Ages to which they inevitably refer as the model period for an ideal society. The assumption is that the subordination of the secular to the spiritual which they (unhistorically) claim to have been the basis for medieval French society can be attained by the reintroduction of a similarly ordered social structure. Not that they suggest the inner problems of man can be solved simply by modifying earthly institutions, but the two must be changed concurrently. Such change necessitated the strengthening of the temporal power of the Church, and maintaining hostility to all forces, such as socialism, that laid emphasis merely on the physical amelioration of man's condition.

Here is the point at which ideals and practice fell apart. It was by no means clear how a hierarchy was to be found capable of assuming the twin responsibilities of material and spiritual leadership, given the irremediably corrupted nature of the upper classes. And, since the nobility and *bourgeoisie* remained almost to a man committed to the Church as a means of keeping the lower classes content with bread in this world on the promise of cake in the next, there was a clear danger of the fanaticism of the revival merely becoming the tool of the traditional Right. An ideology was needed which called for order, hierarchy, respect for tradition and commitment to the soil of France, but one less clearly committed to a given social class than was the parliamentary right wing. For such a broad-based anti-democratic movement with which they could join forces, the Catholic extremists needed to look no farther than nationalism.

NATIONALISM AND THE 'NOVEL OF NATIONAL ENERGY'

The re-emergence of a national movement in the late 1880s was the result of two quite separate forces in French society. The first was the desire to make Germany pay for the loss of national prestige incurred in the disastrous outcome of the Franco-Prussian War, and above all to regain from the Germans the traditionally French territory of Alsace-Lorraine. Patriotism was easily allied with religion, for some sections of the Church had interpreted the 1871 defeat as a testimony of God's anger at the materialism of the Second Empire, and had instituted a veritable cult of repentance—the living memorial to which, Sacré Coeur, is ironically also the best example of the identical materialism of the Third Republic in its most tasteless form. Furthermore, Germany, land of not only Kant and Schopenhauer but also of Luther, was the symbol of that individualism and atheism which were regarded as the greatest dangers to the spiritual safety of contemporary France. The second force was the strong current of anti-democratic feeling that kept in parliament a substantial representation of Bonapartists committed to the principle of plebiscitary dictatorship, and led to the coup-that-never-was in 1889, when General Boulanger failed to seize power purely because of his own lack of initiative. A substantial section of public opinion on both the extreme right and the extreme left felt that the administration of the Republic since its inception in 1871 had been carried out by stockbrokers for stockbrokers rather than in the national interest. A series of events—notably the Wilson affair (in 1887, the president's son-in law had been trafficking in honours) and the Panama scandal (in 1892–3, prominent deputies were involved in large scale corruption)— gave added weight to the view that the amassing of personal fortunes was a more prominent aim among contemporary politicians than the defence of national honour or social justice. Such scandals were a great weapon in the hands of the extra-parliamentary opposition at a moment of economic decline and rising unemployment. It was increasingly easy for agitators to arouse alienated groups by selecting specific issues on which they felt aggrieved, a notable example being the anti-clerical legislation of successive Republican ministries, which could easily be made to seem a series of political measures designed to undermine the support of the monarchist party by breaking the stranglehold of its clerical allies on the education system.

This incipient anti-parliamentary movement lacked only an intellectual mouthpiece, which it swiftly found in Maurice Barrès (1862–1923). In his first trilogy, *Le Culte du Moi* (1888–91), Barrès was apparently developing in prose the cult of the individual which was already dominant in poetry. In *Sous l'oeil des barbares* (1888) the hero, Philippe, struggles to define and protect his individuality under the pressures of a conventional French schooling. Two problems are posed: how to avoid falling into the self-distorting and self-deceiving conformity of the contemptible average person (whom Sartre fifty years later would term *salaud*); and how to encompass the retreat into the self without falling a victim to *ennui* and metaphysical anguish. The initial step achieved is to realise that latent emotions and energies must be activated by direct contact with the realities of life. *Un homme libre* (1889) continues the same theme. Philippe sets out to devise a way of manipulating the inner self so as to remain in a continuous state of mental excitement. He achieves his purpose with a blend of rational analysis and intense meditation. With his friend, Simon, he goes off into the country to explore their response to this new experience. Gradually they find that the method is too cerebral. Everything they can bring to bear, be it their memories of the past or their reading of the great egoists of French literature, is insufficient to the task of protecting the self from fits of debilitating purposelessness. At this point Barrès introduces a significant new idea. He defines the self in terms of a neo-Platonic duality of higher and lower elements; but, unlike Plato, he maintains that the lower, animal instincts cannot be ignored or repressed, as this leads to decadence. They must be encouraged and satisfied separately from the higher instincts. The most fitting area in which to engage them is thought to be the dirt and violence of politics, a commitment to reality, but a decision taken in the name of developing one's own energy, and therefore purely egotistical.

Within the same novel, at an earlier stage, Barrès introduces the other vital concept which will combine with this need for commitment to action to form the basis of the nationalist credo—the concept of *rootedness*. Philippe wonders whether his native province, Lorraine, cannot offer him the special stimulus he requires. His companion rebels against the idea of any kind of submission to popular culture, but Philippe returns alone to Lorraine. There, despite an initial revulsion against its colourlessness, he experiences the entirely new sensation of being the culmination of an

historical and cultural process: not an individual but the distilla-
tion of myriad individuals. He will derive his necessary energies
from the soil and the dead, and in his turn will contribute to the
heritage by the uniqueness of his own personality, a symbiotic
relationship which allows the self meaningful independence in the
context of a new collective identity.

This process of transition from individual to collective values
is completed in *Le Jardin de Bérénice* (1891). Philippe enters the
rough and tumble of politics and experiences the beneficial effects
of commitment to action. At the same time—through the characters of his political opponent, Charles Martin, who represents the
destructive force of scientific and positivist attitudes, and Berenice,
the girl they both love, who is the 'soul' of Lorraine itself—
Philippe is convinced of the need to become the mouthpiece of
the instinctive emotional patriotism of the masses, though this still
serves the egoistic end of stimulating, and thus preserving, the
self.

Barrès, though he clung to the shreds of his individualism,
by the end of *Le Jardin de Bérénice* had enunciated all the elements
necessary for a full-bodied proclamation of the submission of the
individual to the needs of the state. Collectivist doctrine was
fully exposed with his second trilogy, *Le Roman de l'énergie nationale*
(1897–1902)—which reads like an answer to the criticisms of
Meredith's four *Odes in Contribution to the Song of French History*
(1898). The three novels portray the lives of seven young Lorrain-
ers from their schooldays in the Nancy *lycée* through to adult-
hood. The first, *Les Déracinés* (1897) deals principally with the
corrupting power of the French education system, epitomised in
the rationalist teachings of that bloodless Kantian, M. Bouteiller,
and with the further depraving influence exercised by Paris.
The city draws young men of talent away from the provinces,
deprives them of the necessary contact with the historical, geographical and family traditions of which they are the products,
and exposes them to a world where every individual struggles for

himself. The corruption of the newspaper world and of politics are central to the review of Parisian life Barrès offers, but the work is not principally one of social satire. He proposes an analysis of the spiritual and intellectual causes of rottenness in France, and indicates the cure: 'The problem is simply to associate oneself with the national energy, to distinguish its direction and to accept its different stages.' Education is criticised as leading the young precisely away from everything that is essential to the national energy. It exalts mental activity at the expense of practical action; it encourages a rejection of traditional concepts of collective values without offering more than a vague abstract ethical code in their place; it preaches internationalism and idealism without taking into account the determinative force of *race*, *milieu* and *moment* in creating the inner persona of each individual, factors which at the same time provide, he argues, the only meaningful basis for the connexion between those individuals. A conservative regionalism, in which each man recognises the limits imposed on him by family, class and region, emerges as the only basis for a healthy society.

The characters in *Les Déracinés* who survive the test of Paris are those most aware of what it means to be a Lorrainer. They are middle class or aristocratic. The lower down the social scale their social origins are, the greater their corruption will be. Of the two 'scholarship boys', Racadot is executed for a murder contrived in order to acquire the money needed for his newspaper to survive, and his accomplice, Mouchefrin, though he escapes punishment, never rises above the meanest existence in the city underworld. Of the bourgeois characters, Renaudin and Suret-Lefort succumb to the logic of self-interest which their rational training has inculcated in them, and become total egoists fighting for their own ends in the materialist *mêlée*. Only Saint-Phlin, Roemerspacher and Sturel keep afloat, for the reasons directly expounded by Barrès in the novel's key chapter, 'At the Tomb of Napoleon':

'There are key words,' Pascal wrote, 'by which the tenor of a man's mind can be assessed': destiny, duty, cultivation, these indeed were the three terms whereby Sturel, Saint-Phlin and Roemerspacher were to be summed up. Suret-Lefort thought only of appearances, Racadot and Mouchefrin of pleasure, Renaudin of food.

Destiny—the acceptance of one's role in life as predetermined; duty—the acknowledgment of a moral debt to the community; cultivation—the awareness of the values inherent in the environment in which they have been raised; add to these the necessity for action, the harnessing of energy to the practical good of the collective cause, and Barrès's philosophy is complete.

The other novels in the trilogy—*L'Appel au soldat* (1900) and *Leurs Figures* (1902)—expand upon the values proposed in *Les Déracinés*. At the same time, by the use of Boulangism in the first and the Panama scandal in the second, they provide a concrete dissection of those aspects of contemporary society of which Barrès approves and disapproves. The theme of the rise of the Boulangist movement allows him to promote his doctrine of political 'realism', in which the end justifies the means. Sturel, who has remained to the end of *Les Déracinés* too much of an idealist to commit himself to politics, is attracted to Boulangism because of its mass appeal. Since the emotions of the masses are an authentic expression of their roots, in that they have an instinctive understanding of reality, then the political manifestations of mass emotion—of which Boulangism is an example—are explosions of that national energy to which Sturel wants to contribute. But he has to realise that action is not separable from corruption; he is shocked when he discovers that many of Boulanger's supporters are in the movement for personal gain. He is shocked still more when he sees how the general has to compromise himself by soliciting financial aid from corrupt circles. Barrès uses the contrast of these circles, the Jewish financier, Baron de Reinach, and his political puppets, with Sturel, to show that the 'facts' of political existence are more important than ideals, provided that one's aim is the good of the community. His critique of Reinach rests largely on the unacceptability of his ends rather than of his methods; though it is axiomatic for him that a Jew cannot act in the interests of France, since he cannot properly partake of the French heritage. It is a pragmatic lesson which Barrès also applies to Boulanger himself, maintaining that it was the general's attachment to a certain kind of romantic idealism—for example, the refusal to take responsibility for the bloodshed and violence that would be involved in a coup d'état—which prevented him from overthrowing the government by force at the crucial moment in 1889.

Leurs Figures completes Sturel's political education. The development of the novel follows, libellously closely, the course of the Panama scandal, which Barrès uses for an attack both on the manipulation of parliament by Jewish financiers—carrying on the theme from *L'Appel au soldat*—and on the parliamentary system. In his previous novel he had defined the satisfactory functioning of parliament as a stable cabinet, strongly led, and supported by a majority of the chamber—a state of affairs he rightly considered had never occurred under the Third Republic. *Leurs Figures* carries the attack further, portraying the deputies of all parties as self-interested, unprincipled hacks, devoid of all concern for the one serious problem, the unity of France. Sturel, ultimately, cannot come to terms with politics after all. He is deterred from his last 'moral' political act—publishing the list of hitherto unexposed persons implicated in the scandal—by purely personal sentiments. At the same time he realises his desire to publish the list was equally egotistic. His final tragedy is that he cannot, like Saint-Phlin and Roemerspacher, be totally saved, for he remains to the end symbolically rootless. At the moment when idealism in politics and love alike has brought about his downfall, Sturel asks his mother impulsively: 'Why shouldn't we go back to Lorraine?' She replies: 'What for? We no longer know anybody there. And nobody would recognise you, François.' It is the patient Saint-Phlin, working away in Lorraine to get the conditions in education changed, who has made the significant first steps towards the regeneration of France, not the dreamer Sturel.

Barrèsian nationalism was no sport. All its major features were designed to appeal to the current public mood. A good example of that mood was the ecstatic reception accorded to the first night of Edmond Rostand's *L'Aiglon* in 1900. Underneath the top layer of the play, which is a re-interpretation of the Hamlet theme—and at the same time a conscious star vehicle for Sarah Bernhardt—Rostand, the literary neo-Romantic, incorporated a neo-Romantic political message, a reconsecration of the Napoleonic myth. The politics are at times quite explicit—for example, in the history lesson, where the young Duc de Reichstadt puts his masters in their place. The whole play is invested with anti-Germanism, particularly in the portrait of Metternich as a figure of Odyssean guile; with Bonapartism (a reflection of the Bonapartist role in Third Republic politics), and with anti-intellectualism. The little duke himself proclaims:

> *N'ayez pas des pensers de derrière la tête,*
> *Ayez des sentiments, là, de devant le coeur.*

[Do not have thoughts from the back of your head, have feelings coming from the front of your heart.]

It is easy to see how dangerous, in a climate of opinion where such sentimental chauvinism was rife, an alliance between Barrèsian nationalism and the reactionary Catholicism of the revival could become. Their paths were not so very separate. The hatred of materialism and individualism, the mistrust of Jews and Germans, the belief in order and hierarchy are common to both. If Barrès promotes no positive religious stance, he takes the line that Catholicism is an integral part of the inheritance that moulds the true Frenchman, and hence an essential part of national life. Such a doctrine could be readily assimilated to the vision of France as the chosen nation of God promoted by Bloy, Péguy and

Claudel. What was needed to bring together the forces of Catholicism and nationalism was a cause. That cause was to be found in the Dreyfus affair.

LITERATURE AND THE DREYFUS AFFAIR

The facts of the Dreyfus case are difficult to determine, though there is no doubt of the innocence of the accused. In 1894 Alfred Dreyfus, a high-ranking army officer, was charged with espionage on negligible evidence. When it became apparent that a member of the general staff was responsible for leakage of information from the war office, Dreyfus—as a middle-class Austrian Jew in a military body monopolised by Catholic monarchists—was picked by Major Henry, the head of counter-intelligence, as a natural scapegoat. Found guilty of treason by an improperly conducted court-martial, Dreyfus was dishonourably discharged and despatched to Devil's Island to serve a life sentence.

There the matter might have rested had not the continued leaking of information aroused the suspicions of Lt-Col Picquart, an officer rather more scrupulous than Major Henry. From this point the complexities of the plot resemble those of a comic opera. To cover the tracks of their own incompetence and dishonesty, and to save the face of the army, a number of officers, ranging from Henry to General Gonse at the war office and General Mercier, the minister, faked evidence and disguised the truth. The unfortunate Picquart was hurried off into active service, in the hope that fate would dispose of him. It was not until 1897 that an eminent public figure, Scheurer-Kestner, vice-president of the senate, raised serious doubts about the case, but he received a very dusty answer from the government. When Dreyfus's brother forced a court-martial of Major Esterhazy, whom Picquart had conclusively shown to be *a* spy if not *the* spy, Esterhazy was, incredibly, acquitted. After all, since Dreyfus was guilty—he had to be, he was a Jew—there was no point in looking at irrelevant details like documentary evidence, for two men could hardly be found guilty of the same crime. With Emile Zola's consequent open letter *J'accuse*, published in the new left-wing paper *L'Aurore* on 13 January 1898, the case passed into the category of 'a question of principle', where it was largely to remain. The government was obliged to take legal action against Zola. At his trial the judge skilfully prevented the defence from raising evidence for Dreyfus's innocence. The war office made a series of tactical blunders, culminating in the prosecution of Picquart, which led to the revelation that certain key documents were forgeries. Major Henry committed suicide; Esterhazy fled to England. Eventually the case was referred to the appeal court, and in June 1899 Dreyfus was retried before a military tribunal at Rennes. Despite the overwhelming evidence to the contrary, the tribunal returned a verdict of 'guilty with extenuating circumstances'! A presidential pardon was the only way out. For Dreyfus that was enough, but many of his supporters, especially the anti-clericals, saw the whole case as a chance to destroy once and for all the power of the Catholic right wing. From 1899 to 1906 there was a systematic purge of the reactionaries within the army and the Church establishment who had made the Dreyfus affair possible. The process was crowned by the quashing of the 1899 verdict and by the triumphant reinstatement of Dreyfus and Picquart into the army.

The most notable aspect of the affair is the relative unimportance of the unfortunate Dreyfus to his enemies and to his supporters. For, once the issue had become public, a process which took fully four years, it rapidly swelled into a confrontation between those who held that the authority of the army, as symbolic representative of all authority within the state, was of greater importance than questions of individual justice, and those who maintained that there can be no meaningful community where justice for the individual is not the guiding principle by which all authority is activated. The Church was solidly on the side of authority. Its voice was largely heard through the hysterically anti-semitic campaign of Edouard Drumont in his scandal sheet *La Libre Parole*, and through the equally deplorable rantings of *La Croix*, the mouthpiece of the Assumptionist order. Ignorant provincial priests, egged on by unscrupulous persons with an axe to grind, used the case to promote a picture of the struggle between good and evil, in which good was represented by France, the army and the Church, and evil by the Republic, Protestants, Jews and freedom of thought. The doubts as to Dreyfus's guilt, expressed by the bishops and endorsed by the Vatican, passed unheeded in a flood of un-Christian fanaticism unparalleled since the Inquisition.

It seemed a heaven-sent opportunity for those like Barrès who wanted to destroy the parliamentary system and substitute a dictatorship to make an alliance in the name of patriotism. It was no accident that Barrès chose the period when feeling over the Dreyfus affair was at its height to bring out *L'Appel au soldat* and *Leurs Figures*, in which his anti-intellectual and anti-democratic message is well laced with anti-semitism. It is the same system of ideas that he expounds in *Scènes et doctrines du nationalisme* (1902), essays in which the Dreyfus affair, particularly the Rennes retrial, is the central theme. Barrès admitted he had reached his conclusions about the case for retrial before he had any knowledge of the 'judicial' facts. The interest of the collectivity was superior to that of the individual, especially if the collectivity was that noble abstraction, France, and the individual only a Jew. Therefore all things must be judged in relation to the collectivity, and not by abstract standards. It is the relativism of his political attitudes put in a new and even more pernicious form. For Barrès the retrial could only harm the prestige of the army and the legal system, both necessary to the strengthening of the nation against the ever-present German threat. Therefore Dreyfus must not be acquitted. Rather than consider the evidence, he prefers simply to blacken the character of the Dreyfusard intellectuals and politicians, libellously accusing them of self-advertisement to compensate for flagging literary abilities (Zola), paid agitation on behalf of foreign powers (Joseph Reinach) and other totally unsubstantiable crimes. *Scènes et doctrines du nationalisme* represents a fair measure of the intense emotionalism aroused by the case, indicates the deplorable level of yellow-press insinuation at which the anti-Dreyfusard campaign was largely carried out, and is entirely in keeping with the proto-fascist theory of the validity of mass emotions portrayed in *L'Appel au soldat*.

Barrès's closest associate, the journalist and critic Charles Maurras (1868–1952), expanded these ideas, disseminating them through the medium of the Action Française movement, especially its newspaper (founded 1908). There are superficial differences between the two men because Maurras appeals to the classical tradition of 'reason', and places his political ideas in a monarchist framework. Yet the monarch he envisages is little different from Barrès's man of energy, the dictator; and the appeal to reason is specious, for Maurras relies just as much on gut reaction, using reason to give the semblance of logic to ideas instinctively formulated. Like Barrès he is a traditionalist and conservative, seeing order as a sign of health in individual, group or culture. Such order he found to be lacking in contemporary society, blaming its absence on the influence of alien elements—Jews, Protestants, Freemasons—who lacked intuitive understanding of the common French heritage. They were not, in his eyes, susceptible to the stabilising authority of the cultural, religious and political values that could alone regenerate France. For Maurras, Dreyfus was guilty because he was one such alien element; all methods of proving his guilt and maintaining his sentence were therefore justifiable, Hence the article by which Maurras rose to fame; in it he defended Henry's name, after his suicide, on the grounds that his forgery had been a patriotic act. It was an outrageous attitude on Maurras's part but it became emblematic of his whole political doctrine and, through the Action Française, of the doctrines of the coalition of Catholic and nationalist interests which was to survive as the mainstay of the French right throughout four decades until it achieved its natural apotheosis in the Vichy régime of World War II.

However socially significant this conjuncture of the two great collectivist movements was, the Dreyfusards admittedly carried off the palm in the literary stakes. If Barrès preferred to take the Panama scandal as the subject of *Leurs Figures*, it was undoubtedly because in the Dreyfus affair his side had come off the loser. For this reason there is little anti-Dreyfusard literature of any great merit; whereas, in the other camp, we find Zola, Anatole France, Marcel Proust and, surprisingly, Péguy. Zola's *Vérité* is probably the weakest of all his novels, reducing the whole case to a crime which, though vile, will hardly stand duty for an event of national importance. The fanatical denunciation of the hypocrisy and immorality of the clergy, the passionate belief in the virtues of positivist education, the rejection of racialism are all powerful themes, but they do not suffice to create a work of art. For different reasons, Péguy's *Notre Jeunesse* (1910), the most famous of the pro-Dreyfus pamphlets he published in the *Cahiers de la Quinzaine*, is equally unsatisfactory. Péguy was deeply disturbed by the many supporters of Dreyfus who, he felt, jumped on the bandwagon and turned the case of justice for one man into a vendetta against army, Church and aristocracy. He particularly deplored the conduct of the parliamentary socialists under Jaurès. As a consequence he developed a theory of *mystique* and *politique*, according to which all causes, from Judaism to nationalism, have a pure essence that becomes corrupted by the manipulation of the cause for partisan purposes. It is an incoherent, emotionally formulated theory which testifies to Péguy's humanitarianism but says little for his intelligence. The work is further disadvantaged by being couched in a mechanically rhetorical style of the peculiarly monotonous type later favoured by General de Gaulle.

If the Dreyfus affair was not entirely a fruitful source of literary inspiration to Zola and Péguy, it proved entirely beneficial to Anatole France (1844–1924) and Marcel Proust (1871–1921). Proust's use of it in the fragmentary novel *Jean Santeuil* and his masterpiece *A la Recherche du temps perdu* forms an integral part of his view of the nature of society; as such it cannot be dealt with here. Anatole France's contribution lies in *L'Anneau d'améthyste* (1899) and *M. Bergeret à Paris* (1901); the last two volumes of his tetralogy, *L'Histoire contemporaine*; in the short story *Crainquebille* (1901), and in the satirical history of France, *L'Ile des Pingouins* (1908). Defender of intellectual freedom, opponent of all fanaticism and violence, upholder of abstract principles, internationalist (he believed in a United States of Europe), Anatole France is probably the figure of his generation who best represents everything that was detested by both the Catholic revival and the nationalists. When Péguy denounced Catholic moderates, he accused them of having as their sole aim in life 'not to make M. Anatole France smile'. Not that France was originally a democrat; the distaste for the masses which marks his anti-Communard novel *Les Désirs de Jean Servien* (1882) is typical of his political attitudes in the 1870s and 1880s. His respect for tradition and intellect led him to prefer the idea of government by an intellectual élite. However, his prime concern was with justice for the individual. In combination with his dislike of fanaticism and a contempt for the antics of Third Republic politicians—whom he travesties under the guise of satire of the *ancien régime* in *Les Opinions de Jerôme Coignard* (1893)—this belief in the importance of the individual sufficed to make him a socialist (though a non-conforming one) for the latter part of his life, and an ardent Dreyfusard until alienated by the political exploitation of the post-pardon period.

As early as 1890 Anatole France had shown an interest in the welfare of the poor, and had published several newspaper articles criticising the negligent attitude of the authorities. In 1897 he attacked the continuing existence of military courts as a survival from the Middle Ages not in keeping with modern concepts of justice. In the same year the first two volumes of the *Histoire Con-temporaine*, *L'Orme du mail* and *Le Mannequin d'osier*, wrily deflated the Renaissance politicking of the Church. So that, before the Henry scandal, he could be said to have declared his progressive position on issues important to the Dreyfus affair—the negligence of government, the corruption of the Church and the archaic complexion of army justice—without committing himself to a pro-Dreyfus stance. His motives for taking the decisive step seem to have been mixed. Nonetheless, he was a leading signatory to the petition of the intellectuals that followed the publication of Zola's *J'accuse*. In part he felt a natural distaste for popular opinion, which happened to be strongly anti-Dreyfus; more importantly, he had no time for the violent anti-semitism which disfigured the nationalist campaign. On a literary level there was the added incentive of freedom to analyse what was wrong with many elements of French society that had aligned themselves with the anti-Dreyfusards and which he strongly disliked. *L'Anneau d'améthyste* and *M. Bergeret à Paris* are not so much rounded novels with coherent plots and character studies as a series of vignettes of major groups and their response to the affair. Republicans, nationalists, clericalists, the press, the provincial aristocracy, wealthy Jews who have been assimilated into the normal patterns of upper class life—all are scrutinised in turn, and their behaviour gently put into perspective by the voice of the seedy old professor, M. Bergeret.

For a more violent, black-and-white interpretation of the affair we must turn to his collection of speeches incorporated into *Vers les temps meilleurs* (1906). The powers of intellectual and social reaction tried to seize control, he says, 'by lies and acts of violence in support of a crime'. The politicians remained their silent accomplices, few of the privileged classes attempted to counter the barbarian threat, and it was left to the 'robust resistance of the proletariat' to save the day. As a retrospective judgment it reveals, perhaps, more about the shift in his political opinions that the affair encompassed than about his awareness of the social realities underlying its course.

Crainquebille better than any other work shows the degree to which Anatole France saw the Dreyfus affair as symbolic of the moral corruption of contemporary society, for it concentrates on a single abstract aspect of the case—the inadequacy of French law and the crassness of those who administer it. Poor old Crainquebille, the street vendor, has a brush with a traffic policeman, and is arrested for an insult he has not delivered. The evidence of a respectable 'intellectual' witness is ignored, and the victim is condemned on the word of an obsessed policeman whose unreliability is demonstrated in the courtroom. The kernel of the satire lies in the chapter 'Apologia for Judge Bourriche':

> Judge Bourriche is to be commended for knowing how to defend himself against the vain curiosity of the mind and that intellectual pride that seeks to know all. Had he compared the contradictory depositions of constable Matra and doctor David Matthieu, he would have entered on a course where one encounters nothing but doubt and uncertainty. The method which consists in examining the facts according to critical principles cannot be reconciled with the proper administration of justice. If the magistrate had the inprudence to follow this method, his judgments would be dependent on his personal wisdom, which is in most cases tiny, and human weakness, which is ever-present . . . Magistrates must abandon hope of *knowing*, and confine themselves to judging. People who want court sentences to be founded on the methodical examination of the facts are dangerous sophists and treacherous enemies of civil and military justice. Judge Bourriche is too much of a lawyer to make his sentences dependent on reason and science, whose conclusions are subject to endless disputes. He bases them on dogmas, he roots them solidly in tradition, such that his judgments have an authority equal to the fiats of the Church. His sentences are canonical.

As a relentless deflation of the mindlessness of the Law at its worst, *Crainquebille* is matched only by Dickens's *Hard Times*.

By the time he came to write *L'Ile des Pingouins*, France's scepticism has to some extent reasserted itself. This is the history of an entire civilisation—a community of penguins accidentally baptised by a Breton missionary and consequently turned by God into men—which parodies French history from its mythical beginnings to the present day. The function of the work is to attack clericalism and the aristocracy; its focal point is the clerical and royalist intrigues that culminate in the Pyrot Affair. An insignificant Jewish penguin, Pyrot, is convicted of extracting 80,000 bales of hay from army stores and handing them over to an enemy power. It transpires that the hay never existed, but fraud and fanaticism combine to cover up the incompetence and iniquity of the war office and general staff. Though France condemns the anti-Pyrots for their bigotry and stupidity, he is no less strong against those who only join the pro-Pyrot party in order to benefit from the eventual political advantages. The individual injustice is eventually rectified, but the social and economic system that allowed it to happen remain unaltered. The illiberality of the Combes régime and its successors has turned Anatole France's social idealism to a bitter pessimism. It was to remain so in *Les Dieux ont soif* (1912) and *La Revolte des anges*, only to be deepened by his despair at the failure of international socialist pacifism to prevent World War I.

Ultimately France, the standard bearer of idealism and internationalism, considered himself as defeated by the forces of intolerance and social reaction which the Catholic revival and the nationalists represented. He was in a sense right, for the younger generation had rejected his causes as irrelevant. But the espousal of collective values was only temporary too, for Nietzsche and Henri Bergson were to provide the main direction for the future. The whole tenor of the period 1880–1910 is best summed up in a documentary novel, *Jean Barois* (1913) by Roger Martin du Gard (1881–1958); despite its early date, it is very much a twentieth-century work. It combines a study of contemporary events and issues, particularly the Dreyfus affair, with an account of the eponymous hero's odyssey from the religious beliefs of his child hood, through the conversion to free-thinking and doctrines of scientific progress, and back in his declining years to Catholicism. Towards the end of the book, in a section entitled 'The critical age', Barois, who is conducting for his paper an inquiry into contemporary youth, interviews two students. Their replies closely define the spirit of young France in the post-Dreyfus era: the call is for order, authority, energy, but within a democratic framework. Science and religion are seen as necessary to society, though completely independent, and the older generation is condemned as fighting the wrong issues in the wrong way. As one of the young men puts it: 'Today, to those who were not there, the Dreyfus affair seems a confused struggle between fanatics with neither coherent beliefs nor leaders, hurling personified abstracts in each others' faces.'

History was indeed to show that the conflict between idealists and upholders of collective values was the irrelevant last convulsion of a dying age, for the world that begat it was soon to be swallowed up in the holocaust of the 1914–18 War. Yet the political and social realignments brought about by the Dreyfus affair were of lasting significance, and the principles raised by it affected French intellectuals for another thirty years and more. Perhaps it is truer to say that what the Dreyfus affair and the war killed between them was the unacceptable face of collectivism.

Conclusion

To extend, on a comic plane, the Cocteau travel metaphor with which this study began: the explorer who crosses nineteenth-century literature by the traditional path can be said to enter via the steaming jungles of Romanticism, emerge on to the harsh, clear-atmosphered plateau of Realism, with the lofty, somewhat uncharted Parnassian mountains to right and left, and progress eventually into the thick mists and eternal twilight of Symbolism. The bird's-eye-view afforded by an aerial tour serves to correct the over-simplicity of such a charting. Throughout the century intellectuals and artists remained acutely aware of certain essential problems: the nature of man, his relationship with the universe, the guarantees of morality, the duties of the artist. The continual rehandling of the same issues from different aspects gives a remarkable consistency to the literature of the period taken as a whole.

Looking at the problems from a chronological perspective it is possible to show dominant trends in the way they were handled at particular moments. For three or four decades there was a sharp reaction against the application of reason to such matters, and solutions were sought through intuitive appeals to ill-defined metaphysical forces. This is the period of Chateau-briand's redefinition of religious sensibility and of Mme de Staël's championing of German metaphysical systems. In the following twenty to twenty-five years the virtues of scientific method were reasserted and all man's problems subordinated to material solutions which remained nonetheless highly coloured by idealist notions. Positivism becomes entangled with Comte's religion of humanity and Renan's scientism. At the same period a completely opposite stream of thought, which rejects the value of sense data and the traditional methods of interpreting the outward manifestations of 'reality', finding significance only in the subjective vision of mystic forces, keeps surfacing in isolated writers, particularly poets, from Nerval to Baudelaire and on to Rimbaud. The end of the century sees all these forces at work together— scientism in the later works of Zola, total subjectivity in Laforgue, aesthetic religiosity in Huysmans, mystic individual vision in Mallarmé and his disciples. Added to these are the new ideals of collectivism, identified with political and religious reactionary forces, mystical but curiously pragmatic, reaching their natural culmination in the activities of the Action Française.

However, here too there is a danger of accepting an unjustified sense of 'waves of development' represented by definable groups of writers, a sense disguising both the co-existence of minority view-points and the constant modulation of ideas held by individual authors. Leconte de Lisle and Hugo both lived a long time; such longevity, when matched, as in both their cases, by an extensive period of creative production, leads to interesting cultural overlaps. It is, for example, a salutary reminder of the complexities of cultural development that the following all appeared within the space of four years: Leconte de Lisle's *Poèmes tragiques* (1884), Laforgue's *Complaintes* (1885), Zola's *Germinal* (1885), Bloy's *Le Désespéré* (1886), Mallarmé's *Poèmes* (1887), Barrès's *Sous l'oeil des barbares* (1888) and Hugo's *Toute la lyre* (1888–93)— the last title is a French idiom meaning the whole range of poetic emotion etc. Between them these works cover a significant proportion of the themes discussed in this book.

The preoccupations of the age can be defined not only in terms of their intellectual import but also in terms of the practical aesthetic problems and solutions they entailed. The world of the Stendhalian, Balzacian or Flaubertian novel cannot be divorced from the concepts of individualism it contains or from the special methods of fictional construction the authors evolved in order to express those concepts—methods which in themselves relate to issues of subjective and objective reality and to the reader's own perceptions thereof. The same is equally true of the poets, however different the texture of their poetry may seem. The superficial impersonality of Leconte de Lisle's descriptions is an embodiment of his pessimist philosophy, just as in Baudelaire's poetry what the poet calls 'the duality of man' and 'the duality of art' are inseparable.

A further dimension which can bring a closer appreciation of many nineteenth-century works is an awareness of the social conditions that produced them—if only, in most cases, by reaction against society. The main reason for this is the simple fact that the philosophical concerns about the nature of man which underlie the novels or poems are closely tied to questions of practical ethics, the possibility or impossibility of changing society, and the ways an individual can or cannot relate to his fellows without being false to himself. To give one instance—the rise of political collectivism in the form of Barrèsian nationalism and the conflict of values stimulated by the Dreyfus affair—a knowledge of the precise social state of France is essential for a proper understanding of the literature. In other cases, as with Balzac or Zola, it is more a question of how historical awareness can illuminate the novelist's preoccupations. Once these various issues—philosophical, aesthetic and historical—have been grasped, the complexity of the inter-relationship of cultural phenomena becomes increasingly more striking.

The advent of the twentieth century did not, of course, radically alter the preoccupations of French artists and intellectuals. I have deliberately omitted from this volume detailed consideration of certain writers, such as André Gide, who were already, by the end of the 1890s, embarked upon interpretations of life which, though well rooted in the problems of the period, are more coherently viewed as foretastes of later philosophical developments. On the other hand, I have included a certain amount of material, notably from Catholic and nationalist writers, which, though it extends as far as World War I, represents the culmination of essentially nineteenth-century trends. The fact remains that, though definition by dates is an arbitrary process, there is in nineteenth-century French literature a surprising coherence deriving from the tensions between convention and illusion, objective definition and subjective vision, around which the major works are constructed. In that sense one may say, with Matthew Arnold:

> The epoch ends, the world is still.
> The age has talk'd and work'd its fill—
> . . .
> And o'er the plain, where the dead age
> Did its now silent warfare wage—
> . . .
> The one or two immortal lights
> Rise slowly up into the sky
> To shine there everlastingly,
> Like stars over the bounding hill.

Select Bibliography

Political and social history
Cobban, A. *A History of Modern France*, vols. 2 and 3. London, 1963–5
Hemmings, F. W. J. *Culture and Society in France 1848–1898*. London, 1971
Zeldin, T. *France 1848–1945* two vols. Oxford, 1973–7

Literary history
Charvet, P. E. *A Literary History of France* vol IV *The Nineteenth Century 1789–1870*, vol V *The Nineteenth and Twentieth Centuries* 1870–1940. London, 1967
Cruickshank, J. (ed.). *French Literature and its background* vols IV and V. Oxford, 1969

Intellectual background
Auerbach, E. *Mimesis: The Representation of Reality in Western Literature*. Princeton, 1953
Carter, A. E. *The Idea of Decadence in French Literature 1830–1900*. Toronto, 1958
Chadwick, C. *Symbolism*. London, 1971
Charlton, D. G. *Positivist Thought in France during the Second Empire 1852–70*. Oxford, 1959
Delhorbe, C. *L'Affaire Dreyfus et les écrivaine françcais*. Paris, 1932
Easton M. *Artists and Writers in Paris: the Bohemian Idea 1803–1867*. London, 1964
Evans, D. O. *Social Romanticism in France 1830–48*. Oxford, 1951

Furst, L. *Romanticism in Perspective*. London, 1969

Green, F. C. *A Comparative View of French and British Civilisation 1850–1870*. London, 1965

Griffiths, R. *The Reactionary Revolution: the Catholic Revival in French Literature 1870–1914*. London, 1966

Lehmann, A. G. *The Symbolist Aesthetic in France 1885–1895*. Oxford, 1950

Martino P. *Le Naturalisme français*. Paris, 1923

—— *Parnasse et Symbolisme 1850–1900*. Paris, 1947

van Tieghem, P. *Le Romantisme dans la littérature européenne*. Paris, 1969 (reprint)

Aspects of Literature

Baldick, R. *Dinner at Magny's*. London, 1971

Bersani, L. *Balzac to Beckett: Center and Circumference in French Fiction*. Oxford, 1970

Brombert, V. *The Intellectual Hero: Studies in the French Novel 1880–1955*. Philadelphia, 1961

Castex, P. G. *Le Conte fantastique en France*. Paris, 1951

Henderson, J. A. *The First Avant-Garde (1887–1894): sources of the modern French theatre*. London, 1971

Howarth, W. D. *Sublime and Grotesque: a study of French Romantic Drama*. London, 1975

Iknayan, M. *The Idea of the Novel in France: The Critical Reaction 1815–1848*. Geneva, 1961

Larkin, M. *Man and Society in Nineteenth-Century Realism*. London, 1977

H. Levin, *The Gates of Horn: A study of five French Realists*. Oxford, 1963

Lukacs, G. *Studies in European Realism*. London, 1950

—— *The Historical Novel*. London, 1962

Mansell Jones, P. *French Introspectives from Montaigne to André Gide*. Cambridge, 1937

—— *The Background of Modern French Poetry*. Cambridge, 1968 (reprint)

Raymond, M. *De Baudelaire au Surréalisme*. Paris, 1940

Russell Taylor, J. *The Rise and Fall of the Well Made Play*. London, 1967

Index

INDEX

FRENCH LITERATURE
In The Nineteenth Century

COMPARATIVE LITERATURE series

Already published

Italian
by Christopher Cairns

The English Novel: Defoe to the Victorians
by David Skilton

In preparation

American
The English Novel: The Victorians to mid-twentieth century
French Literature: The twentieth century